The Principles That Guide Our Work

"AND WHATEVER YOU DO, WHETHER IN WORD OR DEED, DO IT ALL IN THE NAME OF

THE LORD JESUS, GIVING THANKS TO GOD THE FATHER THROUGH HIM." [COLOSSIANS 3:17]

THE PREEMINENCE
OF EVANGELISM

THE PERMANENCE
OF MARRIAGE

THE VALUE OF
BEARING AND
RAISING CHILDREN

THE SANCTITY OF
HUMAN LIFE

THE RELATIONSHIP
OF CHURCH, FAMILY,
AND GOVERNMENT

The Preeminence of Evangelism

"Now this is eternal life: that they may know you, the only

We believe that the ultimate purpose in living is to know and glorify God and to attain eternal life through Jesus Christ our Lord, beginning within our own families and then reaching out to a suffering humanity that does not know of His love and sacrifice.

TRUE GOD, AND JESUS CHRIST, WHOM YOU HAVE SENT." [JOHN 17:3]

We believe that the institution of marriage was intended by God to be a permanent, lifelong relationship between a man and a woman, regardless of trials, sickness, financial reverses, or emotional stresses that may ensue.

The Permanence of Marriage

"A MAN WILL LEAVE HIS FATHER AND MOTHER AND BE UNITED TO HIS WIFE,

AND THE TWO WILL BECOME ONE FLESH. *So* THEY ARE NO LONGER TWO, BUT ONE. *Therefore* WHAT *God* HAS JOINED TOGETHER, LET MAN NOT SEPARATE." [Mark 10:7-9]

The Value of Bearing & Raising Children

"Fix these words of mine in your hearts and minds....Teach them to your

We believe that children are a heritage from the Lord and a blessing from His hand. We are, therefore, accountable to Him for raising, shaping, and preparing them for a life of service to His Kingdom and to humanity.

CHILDREN, TALKING ABOUT THEM WHEN YOU SIT AT HOME AND WHEN YOU WALK ALONG THE ROAD, WHEN YOU LIE DOWN AND WHEN YOU GET UP." [DEUTERONOMY 11:18-19]

We believe that human life is of inestimable worth and significance in all its dimensions, including the unborn, the aged, the widowed, the mentally handicapped, the unattractive, the physically challenged, and every other condition in which humanness is expressed from conception to the grave.

The Sanctity of Human Life

"FOR YOU CREATED MY INMOST BEING; YOU KNIT ME TOGETHER IN MY MOTHER'S

WOMB. I PRAISE YOU BECAUSE I AM FEARFULLY AND WONDERFULLY MADE...." [PSALM 139:13-14]

The Relationship of Church, Family, and Government

"EVERYONE MUST SUBMIT HIMSELF TO THE GOVERNING AUTHORITIES, FOR THERE

We believe that God has ordained three basic institutions—the church, the family, and the government—for the benefit of all humankind. The family exists to propagate the race and to provide a safe haven in which to nurture, teach, and love the younger generation. The church exists to minister to individuals and families by sharing the love of God and the message of repentance and salvation through the blood of Jesus Christ. The government exists to maintain cultural equilibrium and to provide a framework for social order.

IS NO AUTHORITY EXCEPT THAT WHICH GOD HAS ESTABLISHED. THE AUTHORITIES THAT EXIST HAVE BEEN ESTABLISHED BY GOD. [ROMANS 13:1]

FOCUS ON THE FAMILY

Celebrating Twenty-Five Years of God's Faithfulness

Foreword by Dr. Ted Engstrom   *Introduction by Dr. James Dobson*

A TEHABI BOOK

TEHABI BOOKS

Focus on the Family: Celebrating Twenty-Five Years of God's Faithfulness was developed by Tehabi Books and Focus on the Family. Tehabi Books has developed and published many award-winning books that are recognized for their strong literary and visual content. Tehabi works with national and international publishers, corporations, institutions, and nonprofit groups to identify, develop, and implement comprehensive publishing programs. Tehabi Books is located in San Diego, California. www.tehabi.com

President and Publisher Chris Capen
Senior Vice President Tom Lewis
Vice President, Development Andy Lewis
Editorial Director Nancy Cash
Director, Sales and Marketing Tim Connolly
Director, Trade Relations Marty Remmell
Director, Corporate Publishing Eric Pinkham
Design Director Josie Dolby Delker
Editor Betsy Holt
Production Artist Monika Stout
Copy Editor Lisa Wolff
Proofreader Laurie Gibson

For information, please write: Tehabi Books, 4920 Carroll Canyon Road, Suite 200, San Diego, California 92121.

The paper used in this publication meets the minimum requirements of the American National Standard for Information Sciences—Permanence of Paper for Printed Library Materials, ANSI Z39.48-1992.

Focus on the Family
Colorado Springs, Colorado 80995
www.family.org

President James C. Dobson, Ph.D.
Vice President, Focus Resource Group Kurt Bruner
Director of Admin. (Project Manager) Anita Fuglaar
Senior Art Director Tim Jones
Editorial Director (Primary Writer) Chuck Johnson
Brand Manager Phil Hildebrand

This book would not have been possible without the help of Jim Ware, Don Morgan, Tom Minnery, Reed Olson, Bruce Peppin, and many others who wrote and/or rewrote multiple pages of text; the research assistance of Karen Fischer; the technical support of Bob West; the scanning and organizing of many hundreds of pictures by Mary Norris, Jim Cail, Carol Brown, Doug Canning, Peg Mamalakis, Jan Koenig, Mike Harrigan, Kathleen Gray Ziegler; and the many staff and ministry friends who sent us stories when we requested them.

Library of Congress Cataloging-in-Publication Data

Focus on the Family: Celebrating Twenty-Five Years of God's Faithfulness
    p. cm.
  ISBN 1-887656-75-8
   1. Focus on the Family (Radio program)–History.
I. Focus on the Family
(Organization)
BV656.F63 2002
261.8'3585'06073–dc21

                      2002066463

Printed in China

Artville Stock Images: 216
© Bettmann/Corbis: 199
Carol Lawrence: 161
Comstock: 106, 17e, 206
© Corbis: jacket cover d, 3d, 10-11
© Denis Boissavy/Getty Images: jacket back d, 17a, 22
Don Jones Photography: 167a, 188
Gaylon Wampler: 50, 53a, 69d, 71, 72c, 73c, 91c, 95, 100a, 101h, 104abc, 105, 111a, 113, 118, 119d, 120c, 123ac, 130, 131ac, 133, 136ab, 139b, 140bc, 141, 142, 143abcd, 145, 146c, 147abcdef, 149a, 150b, 151, 154, 155, 157, 164c, 167c, 181b, 186c, 194, 195a, 196ab, 197, 211a, 213f, 214, 222b, 223, 224, 225b, 227, 231b, 235, 236b, 243, 252c, 254c, 262b, 273b
Image Technologies: 275
© Jack Hollingsworth/Getty Images: 108-109
© Jean-Noel Reichel/Getty Images: 29
Jim Whitmer Photography: jacket cover a, 3a, 4-5, 173, 272
© Lars Klove Photo Service/Getty Images: jacket back e, 17b, 84
Lennart Nilsson/Albert Bonniers Publishing Company, *A Child is Born*, Dell Publishing Company: 267
© Louis DeLuca: 182, 229a, 229b
© Mark Segal/Getty Images: 2-3
Michael Wray/Corbis: jacket cover c, 3c, 8-9
Myrleen Ferguson: 156
Neal Lauron/Promise Keepers: 228
Reg Francklyn: 27a, 276
© Romilly Lockyer/Getty Images: 221
Ron Nickel Photography: jacket cover b, 3b, 6-7, 17d, 158, 215
SW Productions: jacket back a, 14, 17c, 126, 17f, 240
© Tom Raymond/Getty Images: jacket cover e, 3e, 12-13
Virginia Dixon: 176

Focus on the Family, Focus on the Family Clubhouse, Focus on the Family Clubhouse Jr., Adventures in Odyssey, and Focus on the Family Radio Theatre are registered trademarks of Focus on the Family.

The terms "*Focus,*" "*Clubhouse,*" "*Clubhouse Jr.,*" "*Citizen,*" and "*Physician*" used in this book are references to *Focus on the Family, Focus on the Family Clubhouse, Focus on the Family Clubhouse Jr., Focus on the Family Citizen,* and *Focus on the Family Physician* magazines.

The terms "*Focus* broadcast," "*Focus* program," "*AIO,*" and "*Radio Theatre*" are references to *Focus on the Family, Adventures in Odyssey,* and *Focus on the Family Radio Theatre.*

The term "Focus" refers to the Focus on the Family ministry.

CONTENTS

FOREWORD

One of the most remarkable and exciting things about the Christian life is how God brings people together to accomplish His purposes. Who knows where a "chance" meeting might lead?

I first met Dr. James Dobson at a lunch set up by a mutual friend of ours, Bobb Biehl, more than twenty years ago. I had known of Dr. Dobson's writings and speaking, but I had never spoken with him.

In the course of our conversation, Jim invited me to join the small board of his recently established ministry, Focus on the Family. Unfortunately, my workload and responsibilities at World Vision were fairly heavy and, although I appreciated the invitation, I did not feel I had time to serve.

A few weeks later, at my invitation, Jim Dobson brought a copy of the newly released *Focus on the Family* film series to our World Vision offices. I invited fellow staff members to view the film with me. The particular segment we watched had to do with the importance of being a father, and I was tremendously moved. Toward the end of the presentation, I passed a note to Dr. Dobson indicating my sense that the Lord was telling me I should join the board.

This was a decision I have never regretted! It has been a most meaningful experience for me to sit in our board sessions over these two decades and to witness firsthand God's mighty hand operating on behalf of this vitally important ministry.

God Himself created our first parents in the

> "GOD, WHO HAS CALLED YOU INTO FELLOWSHIP WITH HIS SON JESUS CHRIST OUR LORD, IS FAITHFUL."
>
> [1 CORINTHIANS 1:9]

Garden of Eden, thereby establishing the nuclear family—one man, one woman, and the progeny from that union—and His plan is best. Through my identification with Focus on the Family, I have become increasingly aware of how important it is to strengthen the family unit, which is under major attack by the enemy.

While standing for family issues, Focus has been guided by several important principles since its inception: its strong commitment to integrity; its compassion for parents and children and its dedication to scriptural family values at every level of our society; and finally its utmost honesty and vigilance in regard to financial stewardship.

This twenty-fifth anniversary book illustrates God's incredible hand of blessing on this ministry. I wouldn't have dreamed twenty years ago that at this anniversary we would be celebrating in four major buildings on beautiful property in Colorado Springs, with over thirteen hundred faithful and loyal employees. This is God's doing, and it is marvelous in our eyes!

This occasion allows all of us to rededicate ourselves to the cause of strengthening families and bringing the Gospel of our Lord Jesus Christ to those who need to hear the Good News. As you read the accounts of God's direction and leading in this book, join with us in giving praise to the One who has made all of this possible. "Ebenezer. Hitherto hath the Lord helped us."

Ted W. Engstrom, L.H.D.
President Emeritus, World Vision

Introduction

Greetings from the staff and board of directors of Focus on the Family. We have prepared this book as a chronicle of the past twenty-five years of ministry, and hope that you enjoy reviewing it. We began our service to families on March 26, 1977, with a twenty-five-minute radio program heard weekly on thirty-four stations. It was a very humble beginning, to be sure.

The past quarter-century, we've seen our organization grow from a small office housing two employees in Southern California to an international multimedia organization based at the foot of the Rocky Mountains, reaching more than 220 million people in 107 countries each day. Along the way, we've had the privilege of laughing, crying, rejoicing, and hurting with those who have contacted us in search of assistance. Our mission now, as it has been from the start, is to share the Good News of Jesus Christ with those who so desperately need to hear it, even as we promote and defend the institution of the family as God has ordained it.

There is a Bible verse that adorns the central hall of Focus on the Family's headquarters in Colorado Springs. It reads: ". . . and all the people were very happy because of what God had accomplished so quickly" (2 Chronicles 29:36, TLB). This passage recalls an experience in October 1979, when the resources to continue this fledgling work were very thin. The possibility loomed that we had gotten ahead of the Lord in organizing it. I felt led at that time to fast and pray for a particular three-day period, asking God to confirm for us that we were doing His will. On the third day, my colleague Mac McQuiston asked if I was going to stop work for lunch. I reluctantly shared that I was fasting, to which Mac said, "The Lord asked me to do the same thing." He had been quietly fasting and praying for the ministry during those identical days. We left together and sat in the car, talking and praying about what the Lord was saying to us. The scripture quoted from 2 Chronicles became our theme verse as we looked to heaven for guidance. The rest is history, as they say. Indeed, the ministry grew exponentially from that day, with the necessary finances and personnel becoming available to meet the needs of thousands, and then millions, of family members around the world. We have never forgotten that inauspicious beginning and how God clearly put His blessing on what He had called us to do.

In the coming years, for as long as God allows additional chapters in Focus on the Family's story to be written, we must remember that this ministry belongs not to any one person or group, but to Him only. As He provides us with the means to come alongside additional hurting individuals and families in an increasingly complex world, our prayer is that, like the Israelites all those centuries ago, we would marvel anew at "what God has accomplished so quickly."

James C. Dobson, Ph.D.
President

> "PRAISE BE TO THE GOD AND FATHER OF OUR LORD JESUS CHRIST, WHO HAS BLESSED US IN THE HEAVENLY REALMS WITH EVERY SPIRITUAL BLESSING IN CHRIST."
>
> [EPHESIANS 1:3]

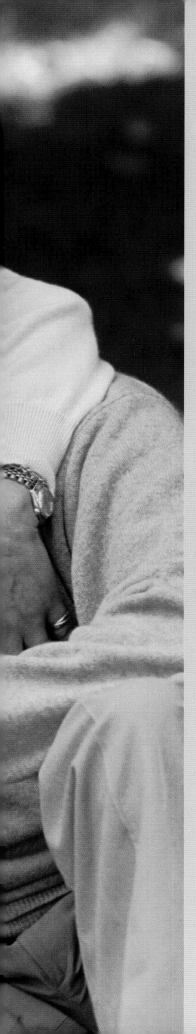

PART ONE

TURNING HEARTS TOWARD HOME

Our Mission and How It All Began

" …AND ALL THE PEOPLE WERE VERY HAPPY BECAUSE OF WHAT GOD HAD ACCOMPLISHED SO QUICKLY."

[2 CHRONICLES 29:36]

Focus on the Family's entire history can be summed up in this simple fact: We have attempted to respond with compassion and care to the needs brought to our doorstep. Twenty-five years ago, Dr. James C. Dobson sensed the Lord's call to communicate a message that would prompt people to return to the biblical model established for the family. The example set by Dr. Dobson's own godly parents, as well as his personal desire to be the husband and father God wanted him to be, were the catalysts that fueled our ministry's early efforts.

As Dr. Dobson began to share his convictions through his writings, broadcasts, and speaking events, large numbers of people responded. His message was one they hungered for, and one that went counter to the permissive culture surrounding them. But people were longing to hear more than just family values—and through the years, many have joyfully responded to Focus's most important message: the story of God's love for every individual and His desire to have a relationship with each of us. We at Focus have the opportunity to demonstrate God's love in everything we do, and we consider that responsibility to be one of the foundational pillars of this organization.

The other pillars upon which Focus on the Family is built include the belief that the institution of marriage is a lifelong relationship between a man and a woman; that children are a heritage and a blessing from God; that all human life is of inestimable worth and significance; and that God has established the institutions of family, church, and government for the benefit of all humankind.

Every year more and more people seek guidance and assistance from Focus, prompting us to add staff, office space, and programs to meet their needs. As God has provided the people and resources to fulfill our mission, we have continued to help those who call on us. The story of His provision is one that never ceases to both amaze us and remind us of our dependence on Him. Humanly speaking, we never could have envisioned where He would lead and how He would use this ministry in His service.

Dr. Dobson addresses a crowd in Denver, Colorado, in the early 1980s.

OUR FRONT DOOR

THE MAIN ENTRANCE TO FOCUS ON THE FAMILY'S Administration Building faces the majestic Rocky Mountains to the west. Those of us privileged to work here draw inspiration from the grandeur of these lofty peaks. The imposing presence of Pikes Peak—which towers at 14,110 feet and dominates the entire city of Colorado Springs—has a way of keeping our humble efforts in perspective. It is impossible to carry on a ministry in this place without being reminded of God's incredible creativity, authority, and sovereignty over all.

This visual symbol of the Lord's awesome power reminds us each day that He has blessed us beyond measure! He has granted us amazing opportunities to participate in His plan by reaching out to more than 220 million people in 107 countries around the world. Day by day He opens new doors for us, carving out a niche for Focus on the Family that is truly global in scope. And yet we

know—indeed, the silent majesty of the mountains will not let us forget—that we are but one part of His Kingdom, just one tiny component of the grand work that His servants have been carrying out ever since Christ walked the earth. Anything we have been able to accomplish or achieve is only a result of His calling us and gifting us with the privilege of serving.

As we celebrate twenty-five years of ministry, we continue to stand in awe and appreciation of God's work, grateful for the opportunity to extend His love to moms, dads, and kids everywhere. ■

The entire Focus on the Family staff congregates in front of the Administration Building in the fall of 2001, at left.

Walking out the main entrance of the Administration Building, visitors to our campus view the front range of the Rocky Mountains, top, which includes the majestic Pikes Peak.

The familiar insignia of Focus on the Family, above, welcomes guests as they enter the campus.

THE LARGER STORY

A schoolgirl bows her head in prayer in observance of the National Day of Prayer in Washington, D.C.

AS EACH OF US JOURNEYS THROUGH LIFE, we tend to behave as though our individual circumstances are central—that we are the main characters in our own earthly dramas. Indeed, we are tempted to cast ourselves in the featured role in the narrative of our lives, while ignoring the "big picture" that encompasses eternity and the billions of people who inhabit the earth.

Scripture teaches, however, that we are people with an Almighty Creator and Sovereign Lord, and that we have been strategically placed within a story larger than our own ... the Ultimate Story.

In His great wisdom and grace, the Author of life has allowed us to be a part of His plan for humankind—to be players within an intricately woven and lovingly crafted plot. Though each of us has an important role, God alone claims the lead. Our responsibility is simply to serve as His supporting cast, trusting Him to bring His promised conclusion to pass.

We recognize that Focus on the Family has been given a unique task within this larger story, and for the last twenty-five years we have sought to fulfill our calling— to draw people into God's family by ministering to individual families. In doing our part, we are granted opportunities to share the Gospel, and, ultimately, to stir hearts toward participating in the greatest tale of all. ■

"The way in which God has used Focus on the Family in my life cannot be gauged. Focus turned an atheist into a believer; revitalized and saved my marriage, which was almost destroyed; and turned our whole family to God—making us a God-centered family instead of a people- or material-centered family." —DIEGO MERA, CONSTITUENT

Our Statement of Faith

We believe the Bible to be the only infallible, authoritative Word of God.

We believe that there is only one God, eternally existent in three persons: Father, Son, and Holy Spirit.

We believe in the deity of our Lord Jesus Christ, in His virgin birth, in His sinless life, in His miracles, in His vicarious and atoning death through His shed blood, in His bodily resurrection, in His ascension to the right hand of the Father, and in His personal return to power and glory.

We believe that for the salvation of lost and sinful man, regeneration by the Holy Spirit is absolutely essential.

We believe in the present ministry of the Holy Spirit, by whose indwelling the Christian is enabled to live a godly life.

We believe in the resurrection of both the saved and the lost; they that are saved unto the resurrection of life and they that are lost unto the resurrection of damnation.

We believe in the spiritual unity of believers in our Lord Jesus Christ.

BEGINNINGS

Jim and Myrtle Dobson, above, with their baby boy in 1936.

Little Jimmy Dobson, left, driving his first "Ford."

Jim officially receives his Ph.D. in child development, at right, on graduation day at the University of Southern California, June 1967.

DR. JAMES "JIMMY" DOBSON GREW UP IN A HOME where Christianity was the foundation for all he was taught. In fact, he has frequently said that Focus on the Family is a reflection of the values and beliefs that were instilled in him by his own parents.

"I watched and learned from my folks as they embodied biblical principles in their own relationship and parenting practices," Dr. Dobson explains. "My dad was a pastor in those early days, and I was greatly impacted by the way he 'walked the talk'—living out his faith at home just as he did in front of the congregation. My mother had a profound influence on me as well. It was her biblically based child-rearing expertise that would later form the foundation of my first book, *Dare to Discipline*. A generation of defiant toddlers has her to thank for equipping parents with the tools necessary to 'shape the will without breaking the spirit!'"

Many people who are unfamiliar with the *Focus* radio broadcast assume that Dr. Dobson is an ordained minister. However, while a biblical worldview pervades everything he does, Dobson has no credentials or training as a pastor, evangelist, or theologian. He was trained as an academic professor and researcher, earning a Ph.D. in child development from the University of Southern California. For fourteen years he served as an associate clinical professor of pediatrics at the USC School of Medicine, working concurrently on the attending staff of Children's Hospital in Los Angeles.

"My years in this institutional setting, which took place in the decade following America's sexual revolution, confirmed what I had long suspected: the family—the very foundation of our society—was crumbling as a result of internal and external pressures on parents and their children," Dr. Dobson recalls. "Marriages were disintegrating rapidly and youth problems were multiplying just as fast.

Once Focus on the Family opened its doors, the Dobsons' influence spread. Dr. Dobson interviews President Ronald Reagan in the Oval Office, above, for an upcoming radio broadcast.

Opposite: Jim and Shirley shortly after their marriage, August 27, 1960. They had "only just begun...."

I became convinced that only a full-fledged return to the Judeo-Christian concepts of morality, fidelity, and parental leadership would halt the erosion of the family unit."

In 1977, Dr. Dobson made the difficult decision to resign from the University of Southern California School of Medicine and Children's Hospital to start a fledgling ministry called Focus on the Family. That was twenty-five years ago, and God has showered His blessings on Focus ever since. Indeed, that humble, "kitchen table" organization has grown into a dynamic, multifaceted ministry that reaches millions of people around the world.

As Focus has become more widely recognized over the years, Dr. Dobson has had numerous opportunities to speak out on family issues beyond the daily radio broadcast, monthly magazines, and other ministry-related venues. Most notably, he has consulted with or served Presidents Carter, Reagan, and George H. W. Bush through numerous government commissions, including the White House Congress on Families, the National Advisory Commission on Juvenile Justice and Delinquency Prevention, the Attorney General's Commission on Pornography, the Commission on Teen Pregnancy Prevention, the Attorney General's Commission on Exploited and Missing Children, the Commission on Child and Family Welfare, and the National Gambling Impact Study Commission.

Dr. Dobson says, "We realize that the incredible growth of Focus on the Family is evidence of the fact that more and more families are coming under fire—and asking for help—as time goes by. As we begin the next chapter in the ministry's history, we stand ready to respond as the Lord provides the resources, guidance, and direction for us to do so." ∎

THE EARLY YEARS

College graduate, 1958.

Jim (standing, second from left) with his college tennis team in 1957. He won the school tournament that year.

Jim served in the National Guard beginning in 1958.

Jimmy at age three.

Jim, age twelve, with his parents.

Shirley at age six.

Shirley, age eight, with her brother, Johnny, age ten.

Homecoming queen, 1960.

Shirley and Jim grew up in different parts of the country. They met at Pasadena College in the 1950s.

Shirley at age eight.

Shirley on her wedding day, August 27, 1960.

A Christian Heritage

THE MINISTRY OF FOCUS ON THE FAMILY is permeated by the wisdom, passion, and spiritual insights of not one James Dobson, but two—for Dr. Dobson acknowledges the tremendous influence of his father, James Clayton Dobson Sr., on his life and views. As an only child, the younger Dobson shared an unusually close relationship with his dad.

"My father's every thought and deed were motivated or influenced by his desire to serve his Lord," Dr. Dobson says. "And I can truthfully say that we were never together without my being drawn closer to God by being in his presence. This was not because he warned or chastised me, but because his love for the Lord penetrated and shaped my own attitudes.

"There is a very real and literal sense in which Focus represents his legacy to the world," he continues. "As a symbol of that fact, a small gallery of his paintings can be seen in the Welcome Center at the Focus on the Family headquarters. Visitors to the campus often ask, 'With everything else he's doing, when does Dr. Dobson find the time to paint?' The answer, of course, is that I don't paint. Those works of art are from Dad."

In fact, James Dobson Sr. was only three years old when he told his parents that he wanted to become a great artist. When he was sixteen, this passion led to a crisis of faith. The high school student heard God's voice saying, "I want you to set aside your great ambition to be an artist and prepare for a life of service in the ministry." Jimmy Dobson Sr. struggled with this conflict for more than seven years, a war between his will and the will of God. During his senior year, he told God that he would not give up his dream.

Dr. Dobson explains:

My dad later described that moment as the most terrible experience of his life. The presence of God seemed to leave him as one person would walk away from another. He later recognized that art had become his god. He chose to sacrifice his faith rather than give up his art. God will not tolerate anything that competes with His preeminence in our lives, and it is not uncommon for Him to test us at the point of our disobedience. My dad failed the test. Seven long years would pass before he would hear that still, small voice again.

Dr. Dobson's father, James Dobson Sr., above.

Opposite: The painting *Man with Helmet* is James Dobson Sr.'s copy of the classic work *The Man with the Golden Helmet* by Rembrandt, circa 1650.

The still life *Medallion*, far left, and the landscape *The Waterfall*, left, were both painted by James Dobson Sr.

Reverend and Mrs. James C.
Dobson Sr. in 1948.

Opposite: Three-year-old Jim
with his father, James Sr.

Jimmy Dobson Sr. went off to the Art Institute of
Pittsburgh, graduating number one in his class. He met and fell
in love with a preacher's daughter, Myrtle Dillingham, who was
also in a state of spiritual rebellion at the time. She had promised
herself never to marry a minister, and she didn't. She married a
burgeoning young artist. On June 13, 1934, the two wed in secret,
but each continued living with their respective parents until
they could afford to set up housekeeping together.

But God continued to pursue Jimmy. A
great spiritual awakening swept through the local
church, which he was not attending. At the urging
of his brother, Jimmy agreed to attend a special
evangelistic service. Dr. Dobson explains the
story of his father's restoration:

> A song evangelist was singing and the words began to speak
> to my dad's heart. Just that quickly, he yielded. After seven years
> of rebellion and sin, it was over. He was forgiven. He was clean.
> The evangelist, Bona Fleming, was unusually anointed of God. When
> the singer concluded, Reverend Fleming leaned forward, pointed his finger
> directly at my dad, and said, "You! Young man, stand up!" When my father
> rose, he said, "I want you to tell all these people what God did for you
> while the singer was singing." My dad gave his first testimony, through his
> tears, of the forgiveness and salvation he had just received. My grandmother
> was crying. She had prayed for him unceasingly for more than seven years.

James Dobson Sr. went on to have a great ministry, leading
thousands to the Lord. God gave him back his art, and He used it to
further the Kingdom. When he died, he was head of the art department at Mid-America Nazarene College, where a building bears his
name. James Dobson Sr.'s grave is marked by a footstone that reads simply, "He prayed." ■

Myrtle Dillingham, top,
secretly married James
Dobson Sr. in June 1934.

Above, the first church
Reverend Dobson pastored,
in Sulphur Springs, Texas.
The church had only ten
members and a budget of
two dollars per week when
Dobson started his pastorate.
Four years later there were
250 members.

THE DOBSON FAMILY

Jim and Shirley begin their lives together, August 27, 1960.

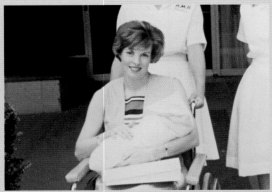

Shirley and newborn daughter, Danae, October 9, 1965.

Ryan and his proud dad, August 30, 1970.

Big sister Danae, age six, and Ryan, age one, in 1971.

Danae and Shirley on a Sunday morning in the late 1960s.

Constituents often comment that they feel as if the Dobsons are part of their families. Here are a few pictures from the Dobson family album.

Ryan at age four.

Shirley and her mother, Alma, at Christmastime in the mid-1980s.

Danae as a teenager in the early 1980s.

Danae's graduation from Azusa Pacific University in 1989.

Danae and Ryan dressed for a formal occasion in 1995.

Jim, Shirley, Danae, and Ryan in the late 1980s.

Dr. and Mrs. Dobson with Dr. Clyde Cook, president of Biola University, at Ryan's graduation in 1992. Dr. Dobson spoke at the commencement, and both he and Shirley received honorary doctorates that day.

"The titles that I cherish most are 'husband' and 'father.' God has blessed me with a wonderful family, and I am thankful every day for the gifts of Shirley, Danae, and Ryan."

—DR. JAMES DOBSON

Jim with Mindy, early 1980s.

The Dobsons' strong-willed dog, Sigmund "Siggy" Freud.

Shirley winds up for the pitch.

Mitzy.

In between the books, broadcasts, and other ministry responsibilities, the Dobsons find time to have fun with family and friends.

Shirley enjoys the California sunshine, mid-1980s.

Ryan on horseback, early 1970s.

Jim and Shirley skiing at Mammoth, California, in the 1980s.

Danae at play in the snow.

Jim Dobson with friends Chuck Swindoll, center, and Peb Jackson on a Canadian fishing trip in the 1980s.

Ryan rappelling down a mountain.

A Spirit Lives On

Jim Dobson with his father and family dog Penny in 1955.

JAMES DOBSON SR. WAS INTEGRALLY INVOLVED in many of his son's milestone events. He performed the wedding ceremony on August 27, 1960, when Jim and Shirley pledged their vows as husband and wife. He served as an editorial adviser for his son's writings, reading the manuscripts prior to submission and then sharing his thoughts with the young author. He also was very involved when his son faced a pivotal decision in the mid-1970s.

"At that time, I found myself at a professional crossroads," Dr. Dobson remembers. "One path led toward continuing success as a member of the staff of Children's Hospital. The other would take me in the direction of ministering to families through books such as *Dare to Discipline* (which at the time had become a best-seller). I would have liked to keep a foot in each world, but knew that this wouldn't be possible without serious sacrifices for my family."

It was at this strategic moment that Dr. Dobson pulled out a letter his dad had written some time before. This, in part, is what it said:

My prayer and hope and expectation is that the same reverential affinity under God will always exist between you and your children [as the one between you and me]. I am very sure that love and faith in a living Christ are the only cornerstones, the only building blocks for the making of memories that bless rather than burn. I'm very happy about your success, which is now coming in like showers. It is important for men, in all vocations, to experience the realization of their dreams. At this point, you have had a very high ratio of positive returns on your endeavors—almost unbelievable, in fact. I don't need to remind you that it won't always be so. Life will test you deeply, if only in the ultimate when we have to lay down everything. We must all pray definitely, pointedly, and continuously for your children. They are growing up in the wickedest section of a world much farther gone into moral decline than the world into which you were born. I have observed that one of the greatest delusions is to suppose that children will be devout Christians simply because their parents have been, or that any of them will enter into life in

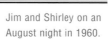

Jim and Shirley on an August night in 1960.

any other way than through the valley of deep travail of prayer and faith. Failure at this point, for you, would make mere success in business a very pale and washed-out affair indeed. But this prayer demands time, time that cannot be given if it is all signed and conscripted and laid on the altar of career ambition.

It was just the word of wisdom that Dr. Dobson needed. Though he struggled with the decision for two years, he eventually elected to resign from Children's Hospital and the USC School of Medicine in order to launch a fledgling ministry for families. It was a small start, but the Lord's hand was in it. In time he and Shirley appointed an independent board of directors, which recognized God's direction to incorporate as a nonprofit organization named Focus on the Family.

Sadly, the senior Dobson would not survive long enough to enjoy his son's new endeavors. Six months after Focus on the Family was founded, on December 4, 1977, James Dobson Sr. was seized by a fatal heart attack. Dr. Dobson's words at his father's funeral speak volumes about their relationship:

Danae and Ryan at home, top, in 1975.

Above, Danae and her grandfather James Dobson Sr. out for a ride.

> So where do we go from here? Do we leave this church today in despair and discouragement? Certainly not, though our sorrow is incalculable. But my dad is not in that casket before us. He is alive, and we will soon see him again. He has achieved the pearl of eternal life, which is our heritage, too. Life will soon be over for everyone in this sanctuary—and for everyone whom we love. Therefore, I have determined to live each day as Christ would dictate, keeping in mind the temporal nature of everything which now seems so permanent. Even in death, you see, my dad has taught me about life. ∎

"When Jim took a leave of absence from USC, it was such a major professional change that he wondered if he was doing the right thing. He had a prestigious position in the academic and medical community at USC, and yet he walked away from it. Nevertheless, I have always trusted his judgment and his interpretation of God's leading in our lives. Looking back, Jim's decision was part of a marvelous plan that we feel resulted from an answer to the prayers of his dad." —SHIRLEY DOBSON

Sowing a Legacy

Dr. Dobson's uncle, Dr. James McGraw, above.

Opposite: One of the final photos of James Dobson Sr., taken a month before his fatal heart attack in 1977.

In 1977—the year Focus on the Family was founded—the Lord made a very important promise to Dr. Dobson's father. The senior Dobson had been praying around the clock for three days as his brother-in-law, Dr. James McGraw, was dying of cancer. Both men were ministers, and James Dobson Sr. was humbly asking the Lord to give them some more time to serve Him and to win people to Christ.

Toward the dawn of the fourth morning, the Lord spoke to Dr. Dobson's father. This, in essence, is what God told him:

I have heard your prayers. I know that you love Me and are concerned for My people and My Kingdom. I have seen your compassion, and I am going to answer your petitions in a way you could never have imagined. You are going to reach literally millions of people for Me, from coast to coast and around the world. But it will not be through your efforts or the work of James McGraw. It will be through your son!

Dr. McGraw died that afternoon, and James Dobson Sr. had a massive heart attack the next day from which he never recovered. He wasn't able to tell his son of God's words to him, but he did share them with Dr. McGraw's sister, Aleen Swann. She conveyed them to Dr. Dobson in a letter in 1985, during a particularly difficult time in which he was questioning how long he could carry the heavy responsibilities of Focus on the Family.

"It was at that moment I realized Focus on the Family is not a product of my creativity or my words or my thoughts or my writings—but that it is God's answer to my father's prayer," Dr. Dobson says. "In one clear moment, I understood why so many doors have miraculously swung open for Focus over the years, and why God enabled us to make wise decisions about the ministry when we didn't even understand the issues at hand."

Indeed, this is not our ministry—the organization belongs wholly to God. It was His idea, and He "owns" it. We are simply stewards of the opportunities and resources He sends our way.

That is why the leaders of Focus on the Family have never sought to stockpile funds for a rainy day. They have based their endeavors on the biblical principle of manna, recognizing that God will provide just what is needed to carry out the tasks He puts before them. God has blessed Focus time and again when resources were thin.

Paul Nelson, former chief financial officer of Focus on the Family, gave annual presentations to our board of directors concerning our budget during his years with the ministry. He would note that our revenue and expenses consistently balanced out—an amazing feat for a ministry largely dependent upon the generosity of its constituents. Year after year, Paul would remark, "We're not that good!" In other words, God knew our needs even before we did, and He inspired His people to give sufficiently—but never more than required—to meet those obligations. ■

The Power of Prayer

It may have been Dr. Dobson's father who received God's promise that his son would influence millions of people around the world, but prayers for His blessing go back at least two generations earlier. That's because Dr. Dobson's maternal great-grandfather, George Washington "G. W." McCluskey, spent the hour between 11:00 a.m. and noon every day in prayer specifically for the spiritual welfare of his family—not only for living family members, but also for generations to follow. In fact, McCluskey died a year before Dr. Dobson was born.

"Toward the end of his life, my great-grandfather made a startling announcement," Dr. Dobson says. "He said God had promised him that every member of the family for four generations—both those living and those not born—would be believers. Well, I represent the fourth generation, and it has worked out more interestingly than even he might have assumed."

All the women in the first three generations married ministers—and the men themselves became ordained! Dr. Dobson and his cousin H. B. London represented the first two members of the fourth generation to attend college. They were roommates, and in the beginning of their sophomore year, H. B. announced that God was calling him to preach.

"I began to get very nervous about the family tradition!" Dr. Dobson says. "I never felt God was asking me to be a minister, so I went to graduate school and became a psychologist. And yet, I have spent my professional life speaking, teaching, and writing about the importance of my faith in Jesus Christ. At times as I sit on a platform waiting to address a church filled with Christians, I wonder if my great-grandfather isn't smiling at me from somewhere. His prayers have reached across four generations of time to influence what I am doing with my life today." ■

George Washington "G. W." McCluskey, Dr. Dobson's maternal great-grandfather, at near left.

Opposite: Young Jimmy Dobson with his mother, Myrtle, circa 1940.

Above top, Dr. Dobson's great-grandfather G. W. McCluskey with his family. His daughter, Bessie (standing, right), married Reverend Michael Vance Dillingham (next to her) and had three daughters (seated from left to right), Loyce, Myrtle, and Lela, who would become H. B. London's mother.

Jim Dobson with his grandfather Reverend Michael Vance Dillingham in 1936, above.

A Book Bathed in Prayer

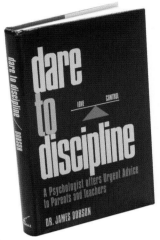

While Dr. Dobson was working at the University of Southern California School of Medicine and Children's Hospital in Los Angeles, he became keenly aware that there was a great deal of confusion and misunderstanding about child-rearing among parents, both Christian and non-Christian. He began speaking to PTA groups and in church services, universities, and family organizations about the principles of child management. He found a surprising hunger for that information, generated by the social revolution of the late 1960s. People had forgotten or never heard what previous generations took for granted. Quite literally, hundreds of speaking requests began to flood in to a man who already had a heavy responsibility at the university. Then one night during a social event, a new friend named Doc Heatherly—who was a publisher and had just heard Dr. Dobson speak— suggested that he write a book on child-rearing. Six months later, *Dare to Discipline* was completed, which has since influenced millions of families. More than three million copies of the book have been sold in forty countries.

When *Dare to Discipline* first came off the press in 1970, Jim and Shirley Dobson requested 250 copies to send to professional colleagues and influential people in the Christian and child-development communities. Jim personally autographed every book. Then he and Shirley packaged them, addressed and stamped the envelopes, and wrote "Special Fourth Class Mail, Book Rate" on 250 labels.

A first-edition copy of *Dare to Discipline*.

The Dobsons saved for two years to make the down payment on their first home, at right. Their Volkswagen was used to transport the first packages of the book to the post office in 1970.

"My father is an Assembly of God pastor, so I grew up on Dr. Dobson's principles at home as well as hearing them from the pulpit. While preparing to become a mother, I read several of his books. Putting Dr. Dobson's principles into practice has been a tremendous help in my own family. People comment all the time about how well behaved our children are, and we owe that in part to the godly wisdom imparted to us by Dr. Dobson. My kids are learning good principles that will carry them through their own parenthood, just as I did." —Deena Rose, constituent

"After that," Dr. Dobson recalls, "we got down on our knees—there in the family room of our first house—and laid hands on that pile of packages. And we prayed. I dedicated the book to the Lord and asked Him to bless this labor of love and use it to advance the work of the Kingdom. Then we carried the packages out to our little Volkswagen, and headed for the post office."

Thirty-two years and one major update (*The New Dare to Discipline*) later, the influence of that book is still being felt. God really does answer prayer! Because of the message of this volume, children around the world have been raised according to a biblical perspective that stands in opposition to the prevailing permissiveness of the last three decades.

One mother wrote to say, "I am a 'Dobson-R-Us' kid. My mother listened to your radio show every day when I was growing up, and she raised me according to the principles you teach in your books. Now it's my turn: I have a strong-willed two-year-old, and I know I need the same guidance that served my mom so well. Two of my best friends agree, so we're tuning in to your program and want to receive the magazine. Thanks!" ■

Jim and Shirley Dobson, opposite, in October 1985.

Above, Ryan plays with the Dobson family dogs, Siggy and Mindy.

DR. DOBSON'S BOOKS

Dare to Discipline (1970; revised in 1992 as *The New Dare to Discipline*)

Hide or Seek (1974; revised in 1999 as *The New Hide or Seek*)

What Wives Wish Their Husbands Knew About Women (1975)

The Strong-Willed Child (1978)

Preparing for Adolescence (1978)

Straight Talk to Men and Their Wives (1980; revised in 1991 as *Straight Talk*)

Emotions: Can You Trust Them? (1980)

Dr. Dobson Answers Your Questions (1982)

Love Must Be Tough (1983)

Parenting Isn't for Cowards (1987)

Love for a Lifetime (1987)

Children at Risk, co-authored with Gary Bauer (1990)

When God Doesn't Make Sense (1993)

Life on the Edge (1995)

Home with a Heart (1996)

Solid Answers (1997; later renamed *Complete Marriage and Family Home Reference Guide*)

In the Arms of God (1997)

Coming Home (1998)

Stories for the Heart and Home (2000)

Parables for Kids, co-authored with his daughter, Danae (1999)

Night Light, co-authored with Shirley Dobson (2000)

38 Values to Live By (2001)

Bringing up Boys (2001)

The poster at right promoted one of the many airings of the successful *Where's Dad?* television special, adapted from film three of the *Focus on the Family* series.

Opposite: Dr. Dobson's desire to spend more time with his family prompted the filming of his final seminar in San Antonio, Texas, in the fall of 1978.

FROM SEMINAR TO FILM

WHILE FOCUS ON THE FAMILY WAS JUST GETTING ON ITS FEET as an organization, Dr. Dobson continued to appear at conferences and seminars around the country, communicating the principles on which the ministry had been based. But overseeing a burgeoning ministry and handling a busy speaking schedule produced a troubling side effect: He frequently came home exhausted, and he began to see the toll this was taking on his wife, Shirley, and their two kids, Danae and Ryan.

"I knew I was at another crossroads, another moment of choice," Dr. Dobson recalls. "As a result, I made a decision that had an extremely significant impact on the course of subsequent events. I told my associates that I was eliminating all future speaking engagements in order to stay home and focus on my own family. After all, what good was the message if I couldn't practice what I was preaching?"

At that point, the publisher at Word Inc. came up with an intriguing solution to the dilemma: He suggested that we film the final citywide seminar and turn it into a series for wide-scale distribution through churches and other Christian organizations. The idea sounded good, but Dobson had doubts. Would people really choose to sit for seven hours and watch a man speaking on film? And would such a seminar be as effective as a live presentation?

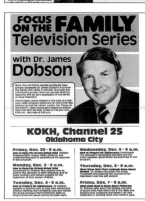

"This project will cost a fortune," Dr. Dobson told the Word executives, "and I don't want your blood on my hands."

Doc Heatherly, the publisher at Word, had no doubts, however—or if he did, he chose to put them aside. So in September 1978, a seminar in San Antonio, Texas, was filmed. The resulting film series, *Focus on the Family*, became an overnight phenomenon, with churches waiting in line to show it to their congregations. The Lord blessed Dobson's decision to stay home with his family by turning it into an opportunity to reach a much broader audience. While he was home with Shirley and their children, Focus on the Family's message was out there on film, touching many more families—an estimated eighty million viewers—than he ever could have hoped to address in person.

A follow-up film series, *Turn Your Heart Toward Home,* was created at a rally in Cincinnati in March 1985. These films, too, have been seen by millions of viewers in churches and small groups around the globe. This series provided Shirley with the opportunity to share her life story—a story of God's power to overcome past heartache and tragedy—with a worldwide audience, thus answering a call she had been sensing from the Lord for a long time. ∎

The posters above were used to promote local showings of the film series in churches and on television in 1979 and the early 1980s.

FOCUS ON THE FAMILY

"I first became acquainted with Focus on the Family when I watched Dr. Dobson's film series at our church. I remember thinking at the time, 'Why didn't I have this practical training when my children were young? Everyone should have access to this instruction.' Later I met Dr. Jim and Shirley Dobson—and we have been wonderful friends ever since. Our desire is to see every family—in this country and around the world—have the opportunity to hear about Jesus Christ and His way for the family. Serving on the board enables me to assist in that goal, and it has been a privilege and great honor to do so." —ELSA D. PRINCE BROEKHUIZEN, CHAIRMAN OF E.O.P. MANAGEMENT COMPANY LLC AND FOCUS ON THE FAMILY BOARD MEMBER

An Evening with the Dobsons

It all began in Fort Wayne, Indiana, on April 28, 1982.

More than nine thousand gathered in Fort Wayne's Memorial Coliseum.

The Dobsons spoke at the Seattle Center Coliseum on October 5, 1982.

A standing-room-only crowd of more than fifteen thousand came to hear about biblical family values in Seattle.

Opposite: Dr. and Mrs. Dobson spoke in Phoenix on September 29, 1983. More than thirteen thousand attended the event at Arizona State University's Activity Center in spite of heavy rain.

In the early eighties, Dr. and Mrs. Dobson began speaking to large audiences in major cities across the country in order to underscore the importance of the family and address problems that were undermining homes and marriages. It was the first time Dr. Dobson had spoken to the general public since the 1978 filming in San Antonio, Texas, and the first time Dr. and Mrs. Dobson had addressed a gathering together.

Dr. Dobson's message on life's true values helped many parents reevaluate their priorities. Shirley Dobson's testimony about growing up in a home plagued by alcoholism provided hope for many in the crowds that attended. These messages and the others that they shared became the basis of our *Turn Your Heart Toward Home* film series, which continued to impact families for many years after the crowds left the arenas.

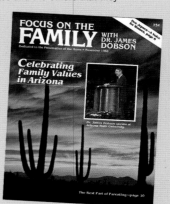

"We decided that the first major event should be in Fort Wayne, Indiana, where there was a bedrock of Focus support. Jim was very skeptical about holding a large-scale event, though. He had never spoken to more than three thousand people at a time and could envision himself being in an eight-thousand-seat arena with a dozen lonely souls sitting in one corner, listening to him and Shirley talk. I tried to put on my best face and let him know it would be okay. And it was. We were inundated with reservations and commitments, and subsequently had trouble fulfilling all the requests! It was an exciting time."

— PEB JACKSON, FORMER SENIOR VICE PRESIDENT OF PUBLIC AFFAIRS

A capacity crowd of more than eighteen thousand people joined the Dobsons in McNichols Arena on April 22, 1983.

People from many denominations and backgrounds participated in our successful Denver event.

In Boise, Idaho, Steve and Annie Chapman and their son, Nathan, sang "Turn Your Heart Toward Home," the title song of the film series.

Shirley addressed the crowd on April 12, 1985, at the Boise State University Pavilion.

Nearly twelve thousand people came to hear the Dobsons in Boise.

Dr. Dobson in Cincinnati on March 8, 1985.

More than sixteen thousand people from ten states packed the Riverfront Coliseum in Cincinnati that night.

The events in Ohio and Illinois marked the end of the "Evening with the Dobsons" series.

Dr. Dobson at the Glen Eyrie Conference Center in Colorado Springs, Colorado.

Released in 1986, the six-part series includes "A Father Looks Back," "Power in Parenting I & II," "The Family Under Fire," "Overcoming a Painful Childhood," and "The Heritage."

Shirley Dobson spoke to the Cincinnati crowd during the filming of Turn Your Heart Toward Home.

Coming Home

Focus on the Family's emphasis has always been on people serving people—not the acquisition of buildings and edifices. Still, the need for a functional, efficient headquarters became more and more acute at each new stage of growth in Focus's history, as staff increased to meet the burgeoning requests for help and resources.

In the early days, the center of operations was quite modest: When Dr. Dobson took a leave of absence from Children's Hospital and the USC School of Medicine in 1976, he opened a two-room office suite in Arcadia, California. He had only one employee, Dee Otte, who served as his secretary/personal assistant from that time until Focus's move to Colorado in 1991. This first office was strategically located next to a post office, which made it convenient to ship books and tapes.

The ministry's weekly radio program debuted on March 26, 1977, and broadcasts were periodically recorded at Whitney Studios in Glendale, California. Before long, Focus on the Family needed more staff and work space to accommodate increasing mail volume. The

organization rented additional office space a block away in 1979 when the team grew to ten employees. But the growth didn't slow down, and employees were soon spread among several other buildings.

In 1981, Focus combined its staff in a newly constructed building at 41 East Foothill Boulevard in Arcadia, which it later purchased. But the ministry continued to grow, and additional office and warehouse space was leased in the adjacent community of Monrovia. Focus added a new headquarters across the street at 50 East Foothill Boulevard in 1984, the first structure actually designed and built for the ministry.

In 1987, after yet another period of extraordinary growth that resulted in staff being dispersed to eight different buildings, Focus began to search for property both locally and out of state. The ministry sold the Arcadia offices and purchased property near California Polytechnic University (Cal Poly Pomona), about twenty miles east of Arcadia. The dedication ceremony for the new headquarters was held in January 1988, just a few months after the ministry's tenth anniversary.

But as before, there were more requests for help, which required more staff to meet those needs. To complicate matters, high taxes and real estate costs made further expansion in Pomona prohibitive. So for the second time in its history, Focus began to explore locations

Dr. Dobson opened his first office, top, at 735 West Duarte Road in Arcadia, California, and hired his first employee, Dee Otte, above. She served as his personal assistant for fifteen years.

Our tiny staff, top left, at Christmastime in 1979. Bottom left: The staff poses in front of the new Pomona, California, headquarters in November 1987.

Opposite: The leadership team (left to right, Gil Moegerle, Dr. Dobson, Peb Jackson, and Sherm Williams) breaks ground on December 18, 1983, for the new building at 50 East Foothill Boulevard in Arcadia.

outside California, considering sites in Raleigh-Durham, Seattle, Colorado Springs, and Nashville. After prayerful consideration, Focus's leaders and board of directors clearly sensed God's direction to move the ministry to Colorado Springs.

Of the nearly eight hundred employees in the California office at the time of the move, about half were able to relocate with the ministry. After months of careful preparation by an advance team, the move began in September 1991. A caravan of more than seventy moving vans made the trek from Pomona to Colorado Springs within one week. Dr. Dobson challenged the staff to get everything ready in temporary locations so that no letter would go unanswered any longer than necessary and no phone calls would be missed. After a great deal of hard work and much prayer, Monday morning, September

21, found the systems up and running, the phones ringing, and both old and new staff at work in the leased offices. The ministry hired more than three hundred people from ten thousand applicants within the next four months.

Construction began on the new campus a year after Focus arrived in Colorado, and staff moved into the headquarters in the summer of 1993. God has provided each new location as needed, from those humble work spaces in the early nomadic years to the beautiful—and permanent—place we now call home. ■

From 1981 through 1987, our staff was at 41 East Foothill Boulevard, top, in Arcadia, California.

Dr. and Shirley Dobson, above, dedicate the 41 East Foothill building.

At right, the Focus staff at the 41 East Foothill building.

Opposite: 50 East Foothill Boulevard in Arcadia, California, was Focus's home from 1984 to 1987.

"I wish I could say that I knew where the Lord was leading when I started Focus on the Family, but that is not true. I simply felt He wanted me to prepare a regular broadcast and to speak to family-related issues. Everything that has happened since then has been a surprise and a labor of love." —Dr. James Dobson

FROM HOUSE TO HOME

Dr. Dobson shares highlights from the first ten years of ministry at the Pomona dedication, January 1988.

Our new headquarters in Pomona, California (1987-1991).

The Azusa Pacific University choir and orchestra perform at the ceremony.

More than sixty-five hundred friends attended the ceremony.

The entrance to the main building in Pomona.

The walkway between the two original buildings in Pomona.

Dr. Dobson dedicates the new Distribution Center in Pomona on October 6, 1989.

The completed Distribution Center.

Looking down on the "hot tub"—the lobby and reception area in Pomona.

The Pomona building, displaying the U.S. flag and yellow ribbon during Operation Desert Storm.

Loaded up for our relocation to Colorado in September 1991.

"When Focus on the Family moved to its facility in Pomona, California, with a staff of four hundred people, I never antici-pated that the ministry would grow much larger than it was at the time. Our efforts were focused exclusively on responding to the needs of the people who asked for our help."

—Dr. James Dobson

"I believe that Jim Dobson has been given to us at a time like this, for a purpose like this. The struggle has already started. The night will be long, the outcome will seem in doubt. But when the dawn breaks, the permanent things of family, faith, and freedom will have won."

— GARY BAUER, DEDICATION SPEAKER AND FORMER HEAD OF THE FAMILY RESEARCH COUNCIL

Early construction shows where the new studio will be.

The Administration Building was completed in 1993.

September 25, 1993, marked the Colorado Springs dedication.

Tony Evans, one of the dedication speakers, rallied the crowd.

More than fifteen thousand guests joined us for the celebration that day.

Dedication speaker and frequent broadcast guest Chuck Colson.

Kay Coles James, another dedication speaker and former Focus board member.

Opposite: An aerial view of the current campus looking north includes the Welcome Center (upper left), added in 1994, and the International Center (at right, behind the Administration Building), added in 1999. The Operations Building (lower left) is not shown.

Our Current Campus

We've come a long way—and not just geographically!

In twenty-five years, Focus on the Family has grown from a two-room office in Southern California with a humble nameplate on the door to a four-building, eighty-one-acre campus at the foothills of the Rocky Mountains. Situated in northern Colorado Springs with a view of Pikes Peak and the Air Force Academy, we have four buildings: the Administration Building, Operations Building, Welcome Center, and International Center. The total area within the buildings is nearly a half million square feet. Things have changed dramatically in two and a half decades!

"In 1976, while sitting in small, rented office space," Dr. Dobson recalls, "I couldn't have imagined the beautiful, spacious campus we currently occupy. But God had big plans for this ministry, and we thank Him for providing every step of the way."

With the help of a four-million-dollar grant from the El Pomar Foundation, land at our current site was obtained for about a dollar per foot. Construction began on the main campus soon after, and the Administration Building and Operations Building were completed, occupied, and then dedicated on September 25, 1993. The Welcome Center, featuring a bookstore and numerous displays for visitors, was added in 1994 (and expanded in 1997 and 2000 to keep pace with growth). But some staff members were still working in leased office space several miles from the campus until the entire Focus team was finally brought together in November 1999, when the International Center was completed.

God's faithful provision for the ministry has been evident: He has provided funds in sufficient supply so that there are no remaining loans on the property or the buildings. Despite the beauty of the structures, they were constructed inexpensively, one of them for only forty-three dollars per foot. The Prince family in Holland, Michigan, gave the primary funds for the construction of the Welcome Center and its later expansion. And two Pennsylvania families, the Bingamans and the Hahns, provided the beautiful red oak that enriches so much of the Administration Building and the International Center. ∎

An interior shot of what our staff calls "Main Street" in the Administration Building, top. Above, a Colorado sunset lights up the Welcome Center, which houses a three-story slide.

Opposite: Classical style is evident in this view of the entrance to Focus's Administration Building.

The stairwell in the Administration Building, far left, shows one of the many verses that adorn the walls of our campus, a reminder of God's provision. Our expanded bookstore, left, makes up part of the Welcome Center.

SERVANT LEADERSHIP

Two FLOORS UP from the main entrance at the west end of the Administration Building is a suite of offices where major decisions are made. The cabinet officers meet each Tuesday morning in the boardroom, and three times each year the board of directors gathers from all over the country for reports and policy-making decisions. Both groups have provided guidance for the ministry since its beginning in 1977. Each board and cabinet meeting includes a devotion from one of the members and a time of prayer and seeking God's will for the ministry.

The hands-on board provides accountability and insight to the executive cabinet, encouraging, inspiring, and motivating careful decisions. Their dedication to the principles of the ministry and to the Lord ensure that Focus on the Family remains true to its calling.

The cabinet officers—executive vice presidents and vice presidents—take responsibility for more than eighty different ministries, from Constituent Response to Public Policy to Broadcasting, Ministry Outreach, and International. The weekly meetings provide effective communication of ministry efforts and synergy within the numerous divisions. ■

The Focus board at a May 1998 meeting, above, in Cody, Wyoming. Standing (left to right): Bobb Biehl, Bob Hamby, Ted Engstrom, Patrick Caruana, and Mike Roberts. Seated (left to right): Tony Wauterlek, Elsa Prince Broekhuizen, Kay Coles James, Shirley Dobson, James Dobson, and Lee Eaton. (Missing from that meeting were Don Hodel, Adrian Rogers, and Steve Reed.)

A typical meeting of the board of directors, left, in the mid-1990s.

Opposite: The executive cabinet handles some preliminary agenda items before Dr. Dobson joins the meeting.

OUR EXECUTIVE CABINET AND BOARD OF DIRECTORS

The executive cabinet (left to right, standing): H. B. London, Paul Hetrick, Jim Jenkins, Kurt Bruner, Jim Weidmann, Rob Flanegin, Stan John, Mike Rosebush, Jim Daly, Ron Wilson, Ron Prentice, Dr. James Dobson, and Tom Minnery. Seated: Yvette Maher, Pam Burnham, Mark Buzzetta, Diane Passno, Tom Mason, and Del Tackett (2001).

Our executive cabinet in the mid-1980s, at 50 East Foothill.

On Tuesday mornings, our cabinet meets to discuss the business of the organization.

Board members (left to right, standing): Anthony Wauterlek, Stephen W. Reed, Lt. Gen. Patrick P. Caruana (USAF Ret), Dr. James Dobson, Bobb Biehl, the Honorable Don P. Hodel, Dr. Michael F. Roberts, and Robert E. Hamby Jr. Seated: Lee Eaton, Kay Coles James, Shirley M. Dobson, Dr. Ted Engstrom, Elsa D. Prince Broekhuizen, and Dr. Adrian Rogers (1999). New board member added in 2002, Daniel L. Villanueva (not pictured).

Our three executive vice presidents: Del Tackett, Diane Passno, and Tom Mason.

The wall outside the boardroom commemorates one of our former board members, Hugo Schoellkopf.

Coming Together

A HIGHLIGHT FOR FOCUS STAFF AND GUESTS is our monthly chapel service—a tradition since 1982, when the ministry consisted of fewer than one hundred employees who gathered in an empty office at the headquarters in Arcadia, California. Our corporate chapel times, as well as daily departmental devotions, have proven critical to maintaining the organization's spiritual health.

Over the years, we've had many memorable chapels. We've had times of insightful teaching from such eminent Christian speakers as Chuck Colson, Dr. Chuck Swindoll, Dr. Ted Engstrom, Dr. Tony Evans, and Dr. R. C. Sproul. We've been moved to action by stirring appeals from Gary Bauer, Kay Coles James, and Janet and Craig Parshall. We've laughed at the humor of Dr. Dennis Swanberg and stories from Patsy Clairmont. And our hearts have been lifted in praise to the Lord under the musical ministry of such notable Christian performers as Steve Green, Michael W. Smith, Geoff Moore, Rebecca St. James, and Steven Curtis Chapman.

Chapel has also provided an opportunity for our staff to celebrate key events in the life of this ministry. We celebrated God's provision when we burned the mortgage on the Pomona property after paying it off in 1989, our second year there. We joined in praise at our first chapel in Colorado Springs after relocating there in 1991. We gathered to pray for the outcomes of the Attorney General's Commission on Pornography and the National Commission on Gambling when Dr. Dobson was a part of those efforts. And we sought God's mercy and protection following the September 11, 2001, terrorist attacks on New York City and Washington, D.C.

We have also commemorated Dr. Dobson's milestones as part of our chapel times over the years. Especially moving and significant was the service in August 2000, when staff gathered to celebrate Dr. and Mrs. Dobson's fortieth wedding anniversary. And no one who was present will ever forget when Dr. Dobson surprised the staff by appearing at chapel—for a time of praise and thanksgiving—one week after his stroke in the summer of 1998.

From 1983 to 1987 Focus chapels were held in nearby churches since we had no single space large enough to bring the entire staff together in our buildings.

Our "Chapelteria," opposite, seats up to eighteen hundred staff and guests.

Dr. and Shirley Dobson share with staff just one week after his stroke in 1998, near right.

Steven Curtis Chapman, middle right, singing in a 2001 chapel.

A Christmas chapel in Colorado, far right.

Hey, THIS IS REALLY LIVING...!
GET A LIFE, Jim!
Chuck Swindoll

I nearly lost my life.. with This kid
man! Just call me "rider".. uneasy
Jim LSDn

Along with celebrating plenty of inspirational and encouraging times, chapel is often just plain ol' fun. One of the most memorable chapels occurred in 1992, shortly after the ministry's move to Colorado Springs. We were still scattered in various office buildings downtown. Dr. Chuck Swindoll, at that time pastor of the Evangelical Free Church in Fullerton, California, was scheduled to speak. As the staff assembled in the First Methodist Church downtown, a loud rumble of motorcycles was heard outside. Everyone inside the church wondered what in the world was going on.

Once the cycles cut their engines, the doors at the back of the church burst open and the employees turned to see the silhouettes of imposing figures in motorcycle leathers. As these characters marched down the aisle toward the front, looking like an invasion of Hell's Angels, the audience was silent until the leader stepped to the platform. When he took off his helmet, there was Chuck "The Sermonator" Swindoll. He had ridden a Harley down from Denver in the company of a Christian motorcycle club.

And the fun didn't stop there. Once the "sermon" was over, The Sermonator issued a challenge: Was Dr. Dobson "man enough" to hop on the back of his bike for the six-block trip back to the broadcast studio, where Swindoll was scheduled to tape a *Focus* radio program? Not to be outdone, Dr. Dobson produced a bike of his own—a ten-speed that had been hidden behind the platform. Its tires were flat and the handlebars rusty. Dobson carried it to the platform and said, "Any wimp can ride a Harley." After the laughter died down, we all exited the church. Dr. Dobson donned helmet and jacket and climbed on the back of Dr. Swindoll's Harley. All of the bikers roared off to the recording session amid loud cheers from the staff.

It's no wonder that staff and guests gather for chapel each month with a sense of anticipation of what might happen! ■

The staff surprised Dr. Dobson on his sixtieth birthday in chapel, above, with a visit from "Tommy Trojan" and a new jacket for the USC grad!

Opposite: Dr. Dobson and Dr. Swindoll pose before riding off on Dr. Swindoll's Harley. Scrawled across the photo are their memories of the event.

Dr. Dobson and Dr. Swindoll in their motorcycle leathers, far left.

Shirley Dobson, near left, tries to prevent her husband from revealing yet another family secret!

FAREWELL TO FRIENDS

ANY ORGANIZATION IN EXISTENCE for twenty-five years has undoubtedly withstood times of crisis and tragedy, and Focus on the Family is no exception. In 1987, four great friends of the ministry—Hugo Schoellkopf, Trevor Mabery, George Clark, and Creath Davis—died in an airplane crash while returning from a retreat at Elk Canyon, Montana. Hugo was a member of our board of directors, and all four victims were close friends of many Focus leaders. In fact, Dr. Dobson had been with the men the night before the tragedy, when they shared a closing prayer together and hugged good-bye.

These men left behind four widows, eleven children, and dozens of grieving friends.

Those who attended the memorial service recall a special moment as they left the church.

Focus on the Family magazine, above, remembers the lives of Hugo Schoellkopf, Trevor Mabery, George Clark, and Creath Davis.

Looking up, they witnessed a beautiful rainbow within the only cloud in the sky. Just above it was a tiny private plane, which was captured on film by one of the mourners. To family and friends who were present, it was a sign of God's love and faithfulness, even in the midst of inexplicable circumstances.

The lives of Hugo, Trevor, George, and Creath were honored in one of the most memorable of G. Harvey's paintings, *Of One Spirit.* The painting features four men riding side by side across a river in a mountain canyon, symbolically representing their crossing the River Jordan. The original of this meaningful work now hangs in the Focus on the Family Welcome Center for our friends to appreciate. ■

The four friends, opposite, enjoy their last evening together with Dr. Dobson at Elk Canyon, Montana, in 1987.

Pictured at left is the "smiling" rainbow and plane seen after the memorial service.

Renowned artist and
ministry friend G. Harvey
pictured with his wife, at top.

G. Harvey presents the
original painting *Of One
Spirit* to Dr. Dobson, above,
at a Focus chapel in Pomona,
California.

Of One Spirit, left, commemorates the four men who lost
their lives in a plane accident
while flying home from a
Focus event in 1987.

G. Harvey's Gallery

A large gallery of G. Harvey's paintings and prints are on display in the Welcome Center. Apart from Dr. Dobson's father, James Dobson Sr., Focus on the Family is probably most closely associated with the Texas painter and sculptor Gerald Harvey Jones, more commonly known as G. Harvey. Mr. Jones, a nationally acclaimed artist whose works have been displayed in the Smithsonian Institution, is a longtime friend of the ministry. G. Harvey's artwork graces our hallways and is featured in a gallery in the Welcome Center.

Nearly every year since 1987, G. Harvey has created a special painting for Focus on the Family, and reproductions of these paintings have appeared on the covers of the December issue of *Focus on the Family* magazine. Prints of this painting have then been made available to readers who contribute to the ministry. These warm, popular prints reflecting family values adorn the homes of constituents who appreciate fine art and the visual reminder of their partnership with Focus.

A Bond of Faith *(1987)*

Heralding the Hope *(1988)*

Charity—The Gift of Love *(1989)*

Building Memories *(1990)*

Whosoever Believeth *(1991)*

Daddy's Priorities *(1992)*

Unto the Least of These *(1993)*

The Blessing *(1994)*

Reflecting His Majesty *(1995)*

A Time of Grace *(1997)*

Ties That Bind *(1998)*

Christmas in the Village *(1999)*

Beside Still Waters *(2000)*

Village Carolers *(2001)*

PART TWO

VOICE OF HOPE

Millions of Lives Changed Through the Broadcast

"FOR WE DO NOT PREACH OURSELVES, BUT JESUS CHRIST AS LORD, AND
OURSELVES AS YOUR SERVANTS FOR JESUS' SAKE."

[2 CORINTHIANS 4:5]

It has been said that God will use any means possible to spread His message of love to the world. At Focus on the Family we can attest to this, since He has used the technology of radio—with its dependence on satellites, transmitters, and digital recording equipment—to reach millions of people around the globe.

Indeed, radio has been and continues to be the heart of our ministry. When Dr. Dobson was first encouraged to take the message for families to radio, he wasn't sure anyone would listen or respond. He needn't have worried, of course. People did listen and respond—by the hundreds, then thousands, then millions. Our initial weekly twenty-five minute show led to a daily quarter-hour program, which quickly evolved into a daily half-hour format.

As our main broadcast grew in popularity, opportunities for other topical programs emerged. New ministry efforts started by Focus often result in new broadcasts, such as *Adventures in Odyssey,* which became part of our outreach to children in 1987; *Family News in Focus,* which represented our voice for public policy in 1988; *Life on the Edge–Live!*, a teen call-in show, started in 1998; *Renewing the Heart,* a program that began in 2000 as a complement to our women's ministry; and *Focus on the Family Radio Theatre,* launched in 2000 to reach a new listening audience through quality family drama.

Other broadcasts present the Focus message in different languages or formats, such as *Enfoque a la Familia* for Spanish-speaking listeners; *Focus on the Family Weekend,* a compilation of the daily broadcasts; and a weekly edition aired on the Armed Forces Radio & Television Services Network, which has been heard around the world since 1983. Additionally, two short features—the ninety-second *Focus on the Family Commentary* and *James Dobson Family Minute*—are aired on many major radio networks, both Christian and secular.

Radio has also opened some doors to the world of television. The ninety-second feature, *Focus on the Family Commentary,* offers insight from Dr. Dobson and is aired daily on major network television affiliates across the United States, including ninety-five ABC, NBC, CBS, and Fox stations.

Dr. Dobson in the recording studio, circa 1987, with Dave Spiker at the audio console.

THE EARLY BROADCASTS

WITH THE PUBLICATION of Dr. Dobson's first book, *Dare to Discipline,* things began to move forward at a rapid pace. The book's common-sense, Scripture-based child-rearing principles struck a chord in the hearts of parents across the country. Not surprisingly, Dr. Dobson became much in demand as a speaker, and he traveled extensively to address church gatherings and parenting groups wherever and whenever the opportunity presented itself.

Dr. Dobson receives the National Religious Broadcasters (NRB) Golden Mike Award at his induction into the NRB Hall of Fame in 1991. In 2002, he received the NRB Board of Directors Award, which honors Christians who demonstrate integrity and creativity and make a significant impact on society.

It wasn't long before several friends started encouraging him to make this material even more widely available...by developing a radio broadcast. It was a great idea. Unfortunately, Dr. Dobson didn't have the financial resources to support a national broadcast, so he approached executives at Tyndale House Publishers with a proposal. He offered them the publication rights to his next book, *The Strong-Willed Child,* in return for a contribution to the nonprofit organization he was forming, Focus on the Family. Tyndale House provided a generous grant of $35,000, and Focus was on its way.

But there's more to the story. The circumstances surrounding the recording of that first broadcast were not exactly what Dr. Dobson had envisioned. He recalls:

> Early in 1977, I received a phone call from TV talk-show host Phil Donahue. He invited me to debate the issue of spanking on his television program. I was not interested, because I had too much to do. Besides, I knew it would be a circus, and I just didn't want to get involved. I told Donahue as much, and he responded by making several promises to me.
>
> He said, "I understand you're with USC School of Medicine. I understand that you don't want to get involved in a shouting match. If you come, I'll treat you respectfully. You'll have an opportunity to speak. We'll set up a respectful debate between you and another psychologist."
>
> I should have known better, but I agreed to appear. I traveled to Chicago and participated in the *Phil Donahue* show. It was an absolute disaster. I couldn't get a word in edgewise until about twenty-five minutes into the program. Even then, Donahue wouldn't let me finish a sentence. I felt manipulated and used. It was extremely discouraging.

Opposite: Dr. Dobson poses with frequent broadcast guest Charles Colson in the broadcast studio, circa 1988.

CHRONOLOGY OF BROADCASTING

March 26, 1977	*Focus on the Family* (weekly twenty-five-minute broadcast) began
March 31, 1980	*Focus on the Family* (daily fifteen-minute broadcast) began
November 2, 1981	*Focus on the Family* (daily thirty-minute broadcast) began
January 2, 1983	*Armed Forces Radio & TV* (weekly thirty-minute program) began
November 1, 1984	*James Dobson Family Commentary* began
November 2, 1985	*Weekend* (weekly highlights from the previous week's broadcasts) began
November 21, 1987	*Adventures in Odyssey* began (weekly)
January 9, 1988	*Family News in Focus* (multiple broadcasts daily on contemporary issues and events) began
February 1, 1988	Spanish *Enfoque a la Familia* began (first international broadcast)
August 5, 1991	*Adventures in Odyssey* moves to daily broadcast
April 5, 1998	*Life on the Edge–Live!* (weekly call-in show for teens) began
January 8, 2000	*Focus on the Family Radio Theatre* (weekly radio drama for families) began
May 6, 2000	*Renewing the Heart* (weekly call-in show for women) began
January 2002	*Focus on Your Family's Health* with Dr. Walt Larimore (weekly call-in show) began

Dr. Dobson left the studio and went back to his hotel room. It was a cold, snowy day. After shutting the door to his room, he crossed to the window and stood watching the snow, pondering the embarrassing episode that had just ensued. Then he began to pray.

"Lord," he said, "why did You let this happen to me? Why did You allow me to come here and waste all this time? Millions of families were watching me. I had an unprecedented opportunity to speak for You and the things I believe. But I never had the chance. Why did You do that to me?"

Dr. Dobson tells what happened next:

The Lord doesn't often give me immediate answers to questions of that nature. But on that day He spoke clearly. Not with words, but with that small inner voice. The essence of what He said was, "Jim, the disciples, the apostles, and all of My followers have had to suffer for being My people. What makes you think that you're any different? If you're going to serve Me, you can't expect to receive a warm welcome everywhere you go. I brought you here to do a job for Me. The outcome is My business now. Let Me carry it."

I heaved a sigh of relief and put the matter in His hands on that morning. I said, "All right, Lord."

Would you believe that on that very afternoon—only two hours later—Dr. Dobson recorded the first *Focus on the Family* broadcast at the Domain Agency. This ever-expanding, multifaceted outreach to families across the country and around the world began on that gray, snowy afternoon, against a background of

Dr. Dobson poses at right with Jon Campbell and Al Sanders of the Ambassador Advertising Agency, which represented Focus from 1979 to 1992.

discouragement and apparent defeat. Flo Schmid, the mother of five girls, was the co-host. Flo asked the questions, and Dr. Dobson answered them—the format was quite formal in those days.

"I soon came to realize that the Lord had not brought me to Chicago for *Phil Donahue,* but for a very different purpose," Dr. Dobson says. "How strange and marvelous are His ways! The radio ministry of Focus on the Family began on that day."

That first weekly broadcast aired March 26, 1977, and was carried by thirty-four radio stations. It was the beginning of a period of explosive growth that would keep Dr. Dobson scrambling for the next seven years to meet the needs that were placed at Focus's door.

In fact, the entire staff has been scrambling ever since. By 1984, Focus had four hundred employees and was heard daily on four hundred stations. Today, the broadcast is carried daily on more than three thousand radio facilities in North America and in nine languages on approximately twenty-three hundred facilities in more than 107 other countries. Who would have thought it was all possible twenty-five years ago? God's grace is truly amazing! ∎

Left, the view from the engineer's console, looking into the Arcadia studio area, where our early co-host, Gil Moegerle, and Dr. Dobson recorded comments.

Below, a popular guest, Dr. Raymond Moore, joins Gil and Dr. Dobson to talk about home schooling.

"Tyndale House Publishers has had a long history with Focus on the Family—actually, from even before Focus began its ministry. In 1976, my colleagues and I had several conversations with Dr. Dobson regarding his dream of creating a daily radio program. Tyndale House finally agreed to make a contribution of $35,000, which provided the seed money Jim and Shirley needed to get the radio program started. By God's grace, Tyndale House had the money that was needed to get Jim Dobson's dream off the ground—and we were happy to give it. What a pleasure it has been to watch the work grow over the past twenty-five years. May God continue to have His hand upon Dr. Dobson and all his associates."

—Dr. Kenneth Taylor, chairman of the board, Tyndale House Publishers

THE BROADCAST STUDIO

MOMENTUM FOR FOCUS'S OUTREACH surged forward tremendously as the radio broadcast became more and more widely syndicated. Even today, with all the other branches of the ministry that are flourishing, much of Focus's ongoing efforts to inspire and inform begin in the recording studio. It is in this state-of-the-art studio—located on the first floor near the main entrance—that Dr. Dobson and Focus staff prepare broadcasts that are heard by approximately 220 million listeners each day.

Visitors to Focus's headquarters can watch a broadcast being taped from the gallery, which seats eighty-two people, on the other side of the studio's soundproof glass. Depending on the broadcast topic, the observers may have an opportunity to ask questions or make comments to the guests. Thanks to a satellite system, broadcasts can be produced and distributed to a worldwide network of stations within hours when late-breaking issues prompt such rapid action.

Dr. Dobson in the studio, above, ready to begin recording another program.

Dr. Dobson and his co-host often meet with the scheduled guests just before the taping, and many of them have commented on his and the staff's ability to put them at ease. This sense of hospitality creates the impression for listeners that Dr. Dobson and his co-host and guests are having a friendly conversation in a living room.

Some weeks are packed with broadcast activities. One such two-day program elicited more than fifty thousand phone calls in the week that followed. The topic was women in combat, its effect on the family, and the safety of families in front-line situations. Some programs have such a tremendous impact that they have been re-aired several times through the years. At other times, friends of the ministry have submitted tapes of presentations they heard at conferences or churches, and the broadcasting staff has reviewed these submissions and presented them to Dr. Dobson for his consideration. ∎

Opposite: The current broadcast studio allows for more guests as well as a larger audience.

Dr. Dobson with Attorney General John Ashcroft, far left, and General Charles C. Krulak, Commandant, U.S.M.C., Ret., near left.

SELECTING THE TOPICS

A Colorado broadcast planning session, above, includes former co-host Mike Trout, current co-host John Fuller, former executive producer Bobbie Valentine, Associate Producer Lisa Cadman, and Dr. Dobson.

At right, guests learn more about the impact of the many *Focus on the Family* broadcasts through an interactive area in the Welcome Center.

ONE OF THE MOST frequently asked questions we receive at Focus on the Family is, "How do you decide which topics to address on the broadcast?"

The answer is fairly simple. We read our mail very carefully, and we listen to what people say about their problems. Then we design programs that speak to their needs. Dr. Dobson elaborates:

Going into the studio, I often have people in mind who are dealing with particular trials. Even though I don't know those individuals, I am thinking about them while we are preparing the broadcast. For example, one day we might talk to a single mother who is facing financial stresses. On another day, it may be a father who is working too hard and ignoring the needs of his family. The confirmation of effectiveness comes when the program has aired and mail and phone calls start arriving from people who say, "I was struggling with that very problem the day I heard your broadcast."

There are even times when it seems as if the Lord chooses the topic for us. In 2001, Dr. Dobson decided to record a program on the topic of embryonic stem cell research. This was at a time when the issue was being hotly debated in our country, and President Bush was not expected to determine his position for a while. But on Tuesday of that week a program was taped, and listeners were asked to pray for God to grant the president wisdom. The program was scheduled to air two days later. Little did we know at the time that on the night of our broadcast, the president would make his historic statement! President Bush pleasantly surprised us by declaring that no federal money would fund further scientific research on stem cells that did not already exist.

"It was a direct answer to our prayers," Dr. Dobson recalls. "I certainly don't think it was a coincidence that we recorded our program at that particular moment in time. God's hand was guiding us every step of the way." ■

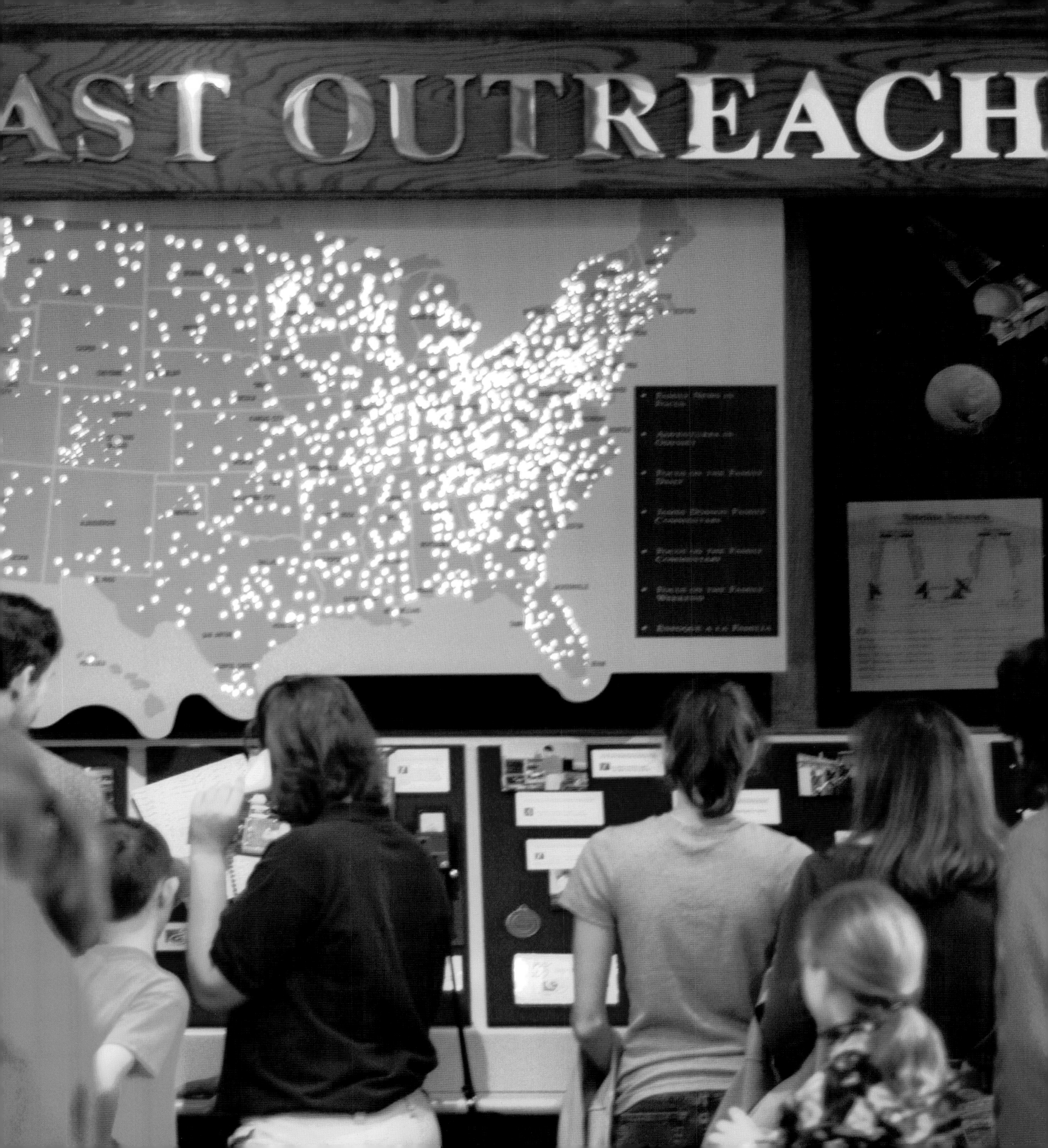
AST OUTREACH

MEMORABLE BROADCASTS

MANY OF OUR CONSTITUENTS want to know which are the best, or most memorable, programs Focus has aired in the past twenty-five years. That is a matter of preference, of course, as most regular listeners have memories of broadcasts that have touched their heart or spoken directly to their needs on the day they heard them. So a more pertinent question to ask is, "Which broadcast has made the biggest difference for you?"

Happy 1st Birthday to the McCaughey Septuplets

For some, the humor of Patsy Clairmont, Dennis Swanberg, and Liz Curtis Higgs have lifted a cloud of gloom. For others, Dr. Dobson's encouragement to recognize that "love must be tough" has inspired them to take difficult yet healthy steps in their relationships, or perhaps his discussions of those times when "God doesn't make sense." And his straight talk on discipline and child-rearing has provided help for parents confused by a society that has moved away from a belief in absolute truth, of right and wrong.

Guy Doud's "Teacher of the Year" broadcast, originally aired in September 1988, highlighted one teacher's efforts to treat his students with honor and respect—and to inspire them to show compassion toward one another. Stephanie Fast's vivid description of her terrifying childhood in Korea inspired those who heard it to celebrate with her the incredible power and love God has poured out on her.

Focus magazine, above, featured the McCaughey septuplets after Kenny and Bobbi McCaughey visited Focus on the Family in 1998 to record a program affirming the sanctity of life.

The *Focus on the Family* broadcast has also featured an interview with Kenny and Bobbi McCaughey, the parents of the septuplets born in Iowa in 1997. The program has hosted the best and the brightest Christian authors and speakers in the world, from Chuck Colson and Bruce Wilkinson to Gary Smalley and Chuck Swindoll.

Some of the most moving broadcasts have occurred when we opened our phone lines for call-ins about particular topics or in tribute to mothers, fathers, children, pastors, or educators. One call-in broadcast at Thanksgiving gave listeners a chance to say what they were grateful for. One girl expressed appreciation that her brother-in-law had talked her out of an abortion. Another member of the Focus family requested a copy of the broadcast tape and gave it to the director of his local Crisis Pregnancy Center. When a client heard the tape, she too made the decision not to abort the child she was carrying. When we hear testimonials such as these, we know we're achieving our purpose. ∎

Opposite: President George H. W. Bush joined Dr. Dobson in a temporary studio in downtown Colorado Springs in 1992 to discuss policy issues that impact the family.

Words of Wisdom

Gary Smalley with Dr. Dobson.

Since the inception of the *Focus on the Family* broadcast in the late 1970s, we've featured a variety of guests and programs. The topics we discuss—from family issues to matters of the heart—are often timeless. This is partly due to Dr. Dobson and our broadcasting team's careful selection of guests and material. Most of the credit, however, goes to our featured guests, who have offered their timely wisdom on a spectrum of subjects. Below are some quotations from some of our most requested—and memorable—broadcasts:

"The Apostle Paul writes that our life is a letter that people are reading. These people would rather see a sermon than hear one any day. They look to each of us, and each of us has the potential to be that molder of dreams." —Guy Doud, "Teacher of the Year"

"Love not only must be confident, but it must be free. Anything that you do that builds a cage around the other person and violates his space, anything you do that puts your clamps on him and says 'Don't hurt me! Don't leave me!' makes the other person desperate to get away. It is simply a characteristic of human nature that we tend to want what we don't have, and we sometimes want to escape from someone who desperately needs us. The antidote to this characteristic is mutual respect between a husband and wife." —Dr. James Dobson, "Love Must Be Tough"

"There are only two religions in the world: Either God is God, or man is god. It all boils down to one of those categories." —Frank Peretti, "God's Way or My Way"

"Jason has brought such sunlight into our home, and to give you an idea of what he's like, I'll tell you what happened to him when he was seven. I sent him off to school one day, and a little while later, there was a knock at the door. I opened the door, and it was Jason. I said, 'Jason, what are you doing here?' He said, 'I've quit school.' I said, 'You've quit school? You're seven years old. You've quit school? Why have you quit school?' He said, 'Well, it was too long, and it was too hard, and it was too boring.' I said, 'Jason, you have just described life. Get on the bus.'" —Patsy Clairmont, "God Uses Cracked Pots"

"If you make the decision to value and honor someone, within a matter of days your feelings will start to change. And that can change the rest of your life." —Gary Smalley, "Incredible Worth of a Woman"

"Several years ago, you aired a show featuring Corrie Ten Boom. I had been struggling for many years with the issue of forgiveness. I knew that I needed to forgive my mom for wrongs done to me in the past, and I really wanted to do so. But although I prayed about it, the feelings of anger and unforgiveness persisted. God answered my prayers the day that I heard Corrie's testimony of forgiveness toward the ex-Nazi who had caused her so much pain. Her prayer, asking Jesus to forgive the man through her, really hit me. I, too, didn't feel I had enough strength to forgive on my own, so I prayed Corrie's prayer. Well, the Lord answered me in just the same way that He answered her—He gave me a heart full of love and forgiveness for my mom." —Sheri Cole, constituent

"I said, 'Norman, listen. I'm your neighbor.' He said, 'I'm your neighbor.' He looked at me out of those thick glasses. I said, 'Norman, do you know who Jesus is?' He said, 'Do you know who Jesus is?' People were beginning to stare. I said, 'Norman, did you ever think about asking Jesus to come into your heart and your life?' He never repeated me. For the first time, he said, 'I've given it serious consideration.' I was shocked." —MIKE ADKINS, "A MAN CALLED NORMAN"

"I'm here to tell you that you're the only one who can choose your happiness. The moment that you choose to be happy, then all of a sudden, everybody else will begin to add immeasurably to that happiness that you yourself, and only you, can ever choose for yourself." —DR. JOHN MAXWELL, "YOUR ATTITUDE: KEY TO SUCCESS"

"I know I'm going through a spiritual battle, but you know what? I know there is victory at the end. I don't live with the hopelessness of thinking it's going to go on forever, and ever, and ever. There are many things that I do not understand...but I know I have an identity with the Lord Jesus Christ. My love for Him does not fail because of the circumstances around me. I may be on sinking sand, but I know His hand is there to lift me up and put me on the solid rock. That's the basis on which I live from day to day." —STEPHANIE FAST, "HEALING CHILDHOOD TRAUMAS"

"[God] gave you that child who's driving you nuts. He created that child before you even conceived what he or she would be like. If nothing else happens tonight...you go home and you tell that child, 'I love you and value you more than I ever have before.' It makes a world of difference if you can realize that...." —CYNTHIA TOBIAS, "NO TWO ALIKE"

"As I was approaching the car, I felt a gun in my back. I turned around, and this man looked at me. He was shaking, crying. He looked like a rabid dog, really. I don't know how to explain it, but he looked satanic. The first thing I thought was, 'You're going to die today.' ...But with my mouth, I said, 'Do you know Jesus Christ?' He looked at me, and he said, 'No, I don't. Get in this car.'" —MARGY MAYFIELD, "SPIRITUAL WARFARE: THE STORY OF STEPHAN MORIN"

"That wiggliness and squirminess and fidgetiness—we see that as hyperactivity. But if you can look at an ADHD child as one who is probably trying to maintain mental alertness, then that fidgetiness makes sense, because we forget that sitting still probably requires more energy than any single thing we do. We require it of children all the time, but even we as adults don't do a good job of it." —LINDA GRAHAM, "ATTENTION DEFICIT DISORDER" ∎

Far left, popular broadcast guest Mike Adkins, who tells the story "A Man Called Norman." Near left, Dr. John Maxwell and Dr. Dobson before a broadcast discussing the importance of attitude.

TOP REQUESTED BROADCASTS

Even though naming the most memorable broadcast is highly subjective, we can quantify the most requested broadcasts over the past twenty-five years. They are:

"Teacher of the Year," featuring Guy Doud

"Love Must Be Tough," featuring Dr. Dobson

"God's Way or My Way," featuring Frank Peretti

"God Uses Cracked Pots," featuring Patsy Clairmont

"Tilly," a drama related to abortion written by Frank Peretti

"I Will Never Leave Thee," featuring Darlene Rose

"Incredible Worth of a Woman," featuring Gary Smalley

"A Man Called Norman," featuring Mike Adkins

"Experiencing a Fulfilled Marriage," featuring Patricia Ashley

"Your Attitude: Key to Success," featuring Dr. John Maxwell

"Healing Childhood Traumas," featuring Stephanie Fast

"No Two Alike," featuring Cynthia Tobias

"Learning to Communicate," featuring Dr. John Trent and Gary Smalley

"Spiritual Warfare: The Story of Stephan Morin," featuring Margy Mayfield

"Attention Deficit Disorder," featuring a panel of experts and parents

SPEAKING GOD'S TRUTH

"Through the years I have looked to Dr. Dobson and his guests for much needed objective counsel and guidance. When I was going through hormonal 'heck,' Jean Lush told me I wasn't crazy. (I bought her book that same day!) When I was feeling overwhelmed and incompetent, Dr. Dobson told me that parenting is very difficult at times, and that I had those feelings for good reason. Focus, you have been a good friend, thank you."

—RENEE DORR, CONSTITUENT

Dr. Dobson with Fern Nichols of Moms in Touch.

Dr. Tony Evans and his wife, Lois, with Dr. Dobson.

Left to right: Interim co-host Gary Bender, Ambassador Alan Keyes, Father Frank Pavone, and Dr. Dobson.

Ryan Dobson joins his dad to talk about the video My Truth, Your Truth, Whose Truth?

Ron Blue with Dr. Dobson.

Jim Ryun and his family join Dr. Dobson in the studio.

Reggie White and his wife, Sara, with Dr. Dobson.

Dr. Neil Clark Warren with Dr. Dobson.

Gary Bender, the Wolgemuths, and Joni Eareckson Tada, with Dr. Dobson.

Dr. Arch Hart with Dr. Dobson.

Mrs. Jean Lush was a Focus guest several times before her death in June 1996.

Reverend Luis Palau.

Dr. Bill and Vonette Bright in the Arcadia studio.

"Both the Focus on the Family *and* Family News in Focus *programs have ministered to me as a parent, wife, and woman in today's world. The radio broadcasts give me the words and conviction to remain true to God's plan and share it with others. They also keep me on course during the times I struggle or doubt, providing realistic answers to my ongoing questions and concerns. It's like having a friend, prayer partner, adviser, and mentor all rolled into one package—someone who will be with me whether I'm at work, at home, or in my car."*

—MELANIE WILLIAMS, CONSTITUENT

Joining Hands

DR. DOBSON HAS OFTEN SAID that since Focus on the Family is only one part of the Kingdom of God, it should make every effort to give visibility and support to other ministries that endeavor to strengthen families. Therefore, the radio broadcast has played a key role in promoting other outreaches that serve the cause of Christ. Some of these ministries include Promise Keepers (Bill McCartney), Mothers of Preschoolers (MOPS–Elisa Morgan), Christian Financial Concepts (Larry Burkett), Encouraging Words (Dr. John Trent), Urban Alternative (Dr. Tony Evans), and Moms in Touch (Fern Nichols).

Another reason Focus is eager to help worthy ministries is because we're thankful for the established organizations that offered us assistance when we were a fledgling ministry, and we want to pass along the favor. World Vision, for example, provided our inexperienced team with advice, computer access, and other help to get us on our feet. Haven of Rest allowed our staff to visit their offices and benefit from their expertise in responding to radio listeners.

We've also joined with other ministries. In the mid-1980s, Jerry Regier launched the Family Research Council (FRC) to provide effective research and sound information on pro-family issues in government. In 1988, FRC merged with Focus on the Family; it became an independent organization again in 1992. Dr. Dobson has served on the FRC board since 1988.

In 1994, Focus worked with a group of other ministries to establish the Alliance Defense Fund, which provides legal assistance in cases defending family values and Christian beliefs. President Alan Sears and the ADF team have successfully waged battles on many fronts—some going all the way to the Supreme Court—to aid individuals and organizations in their quest for fair treatment under the law.

What's more, the idea of home schooling, once considered an unusual educational approach, gained momentum after a *Focus* broadcast addressed the topic with Dr. Raymond Moore in the early 1980s. Now it is a bona fide movement that includes more than a million students. Many families, frustrated with the values expressed in the public schools, drew encouragement from those early broadcasts and decided to pursue home schooling as an alternative. ■

Dr. Dobson, opposite, at a 1993 Promise Keepers event in Boulder, Colorado, shortly before addressing the crowd.

Elisa Morgan of MOPS, above, with Dr. Dobson.

Bill McCartney and Randy Phillips pose with Dr. Dobson, bottom left, after one of the Promise Keepers broadcasts.

"The year 1993 was pivotal in the history of Promise Keepers. That year, Dr. Dobson held a providential interview with me on his program about a new men's ministry called Promise Keepers (PK). A few months later, Folsom Field was filled with more than fifty thousand men from all over the country. For the next five years, PK experienced exponential growth. God used Dr. Dobson and Focus to help launch the PK movement—a movement in which millions of men have since participated and that continues to impact hundreds of thousands for Christ every year." —BILL MCCARTNEY, FOUNDER AND PRESIDENT OF PROMISE KEEPERS

The Unforgettable Kyle West

The verse Kyle holds says it all: "I can do all things through Christ who strengthens me."

WHILE SOME BROADCASTS TAKE MONTHS of careful preparation and coordination, others result from God's serendipity. Kyle West, the son of a Focus employee, was born with cerebral palsy. At a Focus staff picnic, the seven-year-old met Dr. Dobson, who invited him to stop by his office for a visit. Instead of meeting Kyle in the office, however, he took the boy to the studio and recorded a forty-five minute, spontaneous conversation. It turned out to be a delightful and inspirational time in which Kyle took listeners into the world of a child with special needs.

In Kyle's case, he wondered if his disability would prevent him from becoming a missionary. During this 1999 broadcast, he frankly asked, "What could God do with a boy with cerebral palsy?" Since his birth, he'd struggled with multiple surgeries and physical and emotional challenges. But Kyle didn't just want to survive—he wanted to help others, too. As he shared his inspiration to bring "entire countries to Jesus," many listeners came face to face with their own doubts about their usefulness to God. The cleverness and openness of this boy not only made people laugh but showed them truth as well: that God can accomplish anything with us if we are willing to be used.

Focus received many letters from listeners who were usually unable to tune in to the program due to work constraints or other obligations during broadcast times but found themselves in their cars—at just the right time—to hear Kyle's conversation. Many listened two and three times. The tape of this broadcast went out to Sunday school classes, and hundreds of children wanted Kyle as a pen pal. He told his father, "These people are going Kyle crazy!"

As a Focus publication put it:

It seems God had something to say to His people. And He used Kyle West to do it. The truth is, Kyle is already a missionary. He was sent to tell us to keep going, to not dwell on our circumstances, to eat more ice cream, to make a new friend who needs a hug, to believe that the only ability God needs is availability. The "dis" part excludes no one. "Why would anyone wanna talk to me?" Kyle still asks. Because life looks very different after listening to you, Kyle. Thanks. Things are looking more hopeful by the minute. ■

Kyle alone and with Dr. Dobson, left, following his 1999 broadcast.

Opposite: Kyle's family includes his mom, Sue; brother, Jonathan; sister, Monica; and dad, Bob West, who works at Focus.

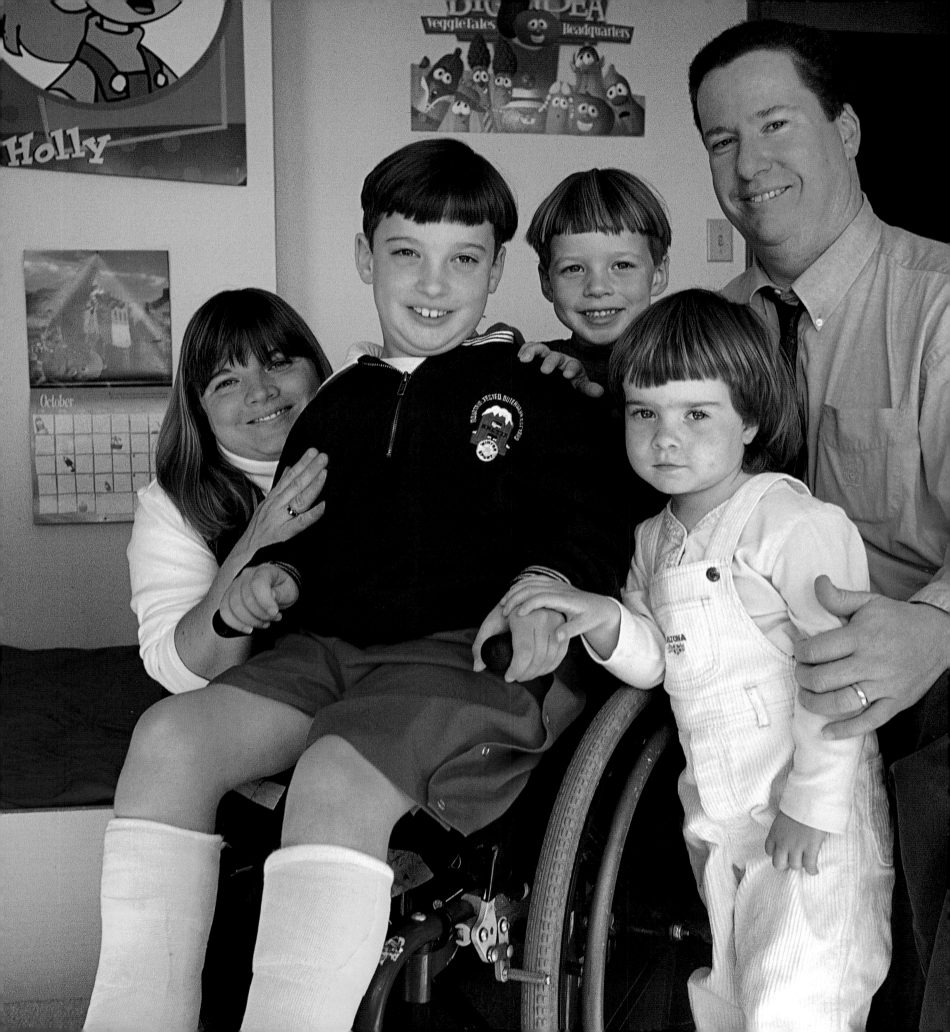

A HEALING TALE

ORIGINALLY PRODUCED IN AUGUST 1987, the broadcast "Tilly" touched many, many hearts. This radio drama, created by Frank Peretti, explored the issue of abortion from the viewpoint of the aborted child. The forgiveness Tilly's mother experiences when she dreams about a meeting with her aborted daughter, now in heaven, has provided hope and healing for many post-abortive women in the years since this story first aired.

One listener wrote: "I felt the Holy Spirit's message strongly when I listened to the story of 'Tilly.' At sixteen, I made an uneducated choice to have an abortion. What was supposed to be a simple procedure turned out to be the most traumatic experience of my life. I lost the baby at home and saw the pain and anguish that my baby had gone through. For thirteen years, I have carried this pain. I went to counseling and heard sermons on forgiveness, but nothing had really touched me before now. For the first time, I truly heard and felt not only what the Spirit was saying to me, but also what my child was saying. I cried tears of gratitude, freedom, and love."

Letters like this are especially meaningful given that Dr. Dobson has vocally defended the preborn throughout the history of the ministry. Many broadcasts, magazine articles, and public policy efforts have focused on the sanctity of human life. But this topic is not purely an academic or policy issue—it involves the welfare of human beings in every stage of existence. Another listener wrote to share her story:

When I was expecting our first child, my doctor told me there was a chance that the baby had Down's syndrome, and he encouraged me to end the pregnancy. I was frightened but stated emphatically that I would not abort my child. My husband was not a believer and was uncertain about my decision.

A few days afterward, Focus aired a program that presented the perspective of a baby being aborted. My husband heard the program and was in tears when I came home. He, too, came to the realization that we should not abort the child. Our son was born healthy and normal, and I have used his story many times to share my faith with others. I thank God for His divine timing and intervention, and I thank Focus for being the tool He used! ∎

The image at top was designed for January 2002 Sanctity of Life bulletin inserts, video covers, and several other resources by Peak Creative, Focus's in-house creative group.

Above, Frank Peretti, broadcast guest, chapel speaker, and conference speaker.

Each January during Sanctity of Life month, *Focus* magazine affirms the pro-life message.

CHANGED LIVES

Focus on the Family has a broad base of constituents. We hear from troubled teens, prisoners, missionaries in Third World countries, suburban families, and single parents.

ALTHOUGH THE RADIO BROADCAST OFTEN RELATES to the specific needs and concerns of marriage and parenting, the primary reason Focus on the Family exists is to spread the Gospel of Christ. While practical problem-solving can assist in the here and now, a relationship with Jesus Christ makes an eternal difference. One young man contacted the ministry with a letter of thanks about how a broadcast had affected his life and many others along the way:

> I began smoking pot with my cousins at the age of eleven. By the time I was nineteen, most of my friends were in jail, and I was a thief, liar, and drug addict. My aunt heard a *Focus* broadcast that described an adolescent drug and alcohol treatment program. My cousin enrolled, and his life was changed forever. Not only was he saved from drug addiction, but he also came to the saving knowledge of Jesus Christ. I signed into the program, too, and so did another cousin, who was heavily involved in drug dealing.
>
> Our family has been saved from the insanity and heartbreak of drug addiction, and we all came to know Christ as Savior, all because you allowed the Lord to use you and your show. And since all three of us are involved in ministry now, who knows how many people have been affected by that single broadcast?

Many other letters and calls we receive describe how listeners "just happened" to discover the *Focus* broadcast. One constituent described the first time she rather unexpectedly encountered Dr. Dobson's advice:

> My oldest son was twelve and a difficult preteen. As I was traveling down the road in an old car listening to a rock 'n' roll station, I was asking God, "What in the world am I going to do with that boy?" I hit a pothole in the road and lost my radio station. I had never heard of Dr. Dobson before, but there he was on my radio talking about a "strong-willed child." I was amazed because he was describing my son as if he knew him.

Another gentleman called to say that he and his wife had been in the midst of divorce proceedings. One day he was "spinning the radio dial" (in the days before push buttons) in an aimless search for help. He "happened on" the *Focus* program, called, and received a referral to speak with one of our counselors. The resulting conversation provided insights and resources that the Lord used to lead the couple to complete reconciliation! Some may call it coincidence, but God's providence would be a better explanation. ■

"It was really through your radio ministry and prayer that God worked in my life and I came to know the Lord. When I think back over all the excellent broadcasts and people I feel I've come to know, it is overwhelming to realize what God has done with your ministry. Your broadcasts have been such an encouragement to me, and have profoundly changed my life. It is a perpetual joy to hear these nourishing words each morning on your program." —ANONYMOUS CONSTITUENT

ADVENTURES IN ODYSSEY

FOR SOME OF OUR CONSTITUENTS under the age of twelve, there is one Focus on the Family personality more widely recognized than Dr. James Dobson. His name is John Avery Whittaker, and he doesn't really exist. But don't tell the children that, because the wisdom he dispenses in the *Adventures in Odyssey* radio program, audiocassette and video series, books, games, and even a CD-ROM makes sense to them—and his wisdom is based on biblical truth.

The *Adventures in Odyssey* (*AIO*) radio program began on a weekly basis in November 1987. Originally titled *Odyssey USA,* its vision was to revive the old-time radio drama, inviting families to listen together, use their imagination to envision the scenes and characters, wrestle with real-life issues facing children, and instill Christian values.

The radio dramas became a daily program in 1992, and there are now more than 450 episodes in all (with more continually being developed and recorded). Characters such as John Avery Whittaker ("Whit"), Eugene Meltsner, Connie Kendall, Bart Rathbone, Tom Riley, the Barclay family, and many others have become welcome guests in homes across the nation and around the world. The stories are not all set in Odyssey, though. Modern-day settings sometimes blend with historical occurrences and Bible days through the ingenuity of Whit's Imagination Station.

Adventures in Odyssey programs are so popular that several dozen collections of six audiocassettes have been compiled. One bedraggled father, with his five young children hovering nearby, approached the Focus table at a home schooling convention. He was carrying six of the cassette albums and wanted to purchase them. When a Focus staff person mentioned that he had thirty-six hours of listening pleasure in his hands, he had a four-word reply. Looking at his brood, he responded simply,

Just a few of the dozens of *AIO* audio albums, popular with kids of all ages!

Opposite: A portrait of John Avery Whittaker, a.k.a. "Whit."

"My son has gone to bed listening to Adventures in Odyssey *every night—every night, that is, following a day in which he has behaved moderately well—since he was two years of age. We own every episode. I do not trust my son to a baby-sitter, but I am enthusiastic about letting* Adventures in Odyssey *lull him to sleep every evening. I look at it as the best investment I could ever make. I already see the results of such good teaching and entertainment in his life. My wife and I looked for something that would reinforce our parenting, and this is it."* —RODNEY WITTLER, CONSTITUENT

"Cross-country car trip." Nothing else needed to be said.

For kids (and parents) who can't get enough of Whit, Eugene, Connie, and the rest of the gang, the world of *AIO* continues to expand. In 1991 *AIO* branched out into video, and as of April 2002, sixteen video episodes were available. The *Adventures in Odyssey* web site is one of the most popular of the Focus online sites. What's more, the "Odyssey Scoop" is a regular column in *Clubhouse* magazine, and *The Complete Guide to Adventures in Odyssey* (an everything-you-always-wanted-to-know volume) was published in 1997.

Adventures in Odyssey fans who visit the Focus campus enjoy a real treat: The lower level of the Welcome Center features a representation of Whit's End—the ice cream emporium and activity center where many of the adventures occur on the radio shows and videos. Fortunate children may even meet the characters of Whit and Dylan as they wander through the play area. ∎

Whit works the counter at Whit's End, the ice cream shop and discovery emporium.

At top, Paul Herlinger, the voice of Whit, stands next to his animated counterpart.

Opposite: Dr. Dobson enjoys a conversation with some friends in the real Whit's End Soda Shop—downstairs in the Welcome Center at Focus.

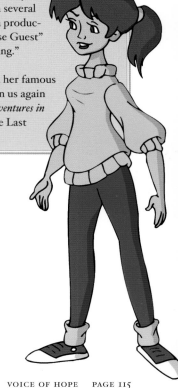

At left is an aerial view of the town of Odyssey. Look closely and you'll spot Whit and Dylan in the Strata-Flyer, with Eugene at the helm.

Connie Kendall, right, is one of the most popular characters in *AIO.* A curious and outspoken teenager, she's been working at Whit's End almost since the beginning of the show.

Hal Smith (left), the original voice of Whit, with Chuck Bolte, former executive producer for AIO and the voice of George Barclay.

The AIO gang. Back row: Jonathan Crowe (sound designer), Marshal Younger (writer), Rob Jorgensen and Mark Drury (sound designers), and John Fornof (writer). Seated: Kathy Wierenga (writer) and Chris McDonald (production coordinator).

"Hi, this is Chris!" Chris Lansdowne, the perky announcer for Adventures in Odyssey.

The Barclay family, played by David Griffin ("Jimmy"), Azure Janosky ("Donna"), Chuck Bolte ("George"), and Carol Bilger ("Mary").

"In the course of our noteworthy tenure with Adventures in Odyssey, *it truly is a wonder to observe how God has utilized the serial in such a manner as to influence the younger members of our population for His greater purposes!"*

— **Eugene Meltsner, Odyssey resident**

Left to right: Alan Young ("Jack"), Ed Walker ("Tom"), Mark Drury (sound designer), Katie Leigh Pavlakovich ("Connie"), Dave Madden ("Bernard"), Dave Arnold (sound designer), and Paul McCusker (executive producer).

"What Eugene said was, 'We think it's wonderful to see how God has used Adventures in Odyssey *over the years to impact the lives of kids for His glory.' By the way, I heartily agree with Eugene. And it's my hope that each program will continue to draw kids closer to God and His adventure for their lives."*

—JOHN AVERY WHITTAKER ("WHIT"), ODYSSEY RESIDENT

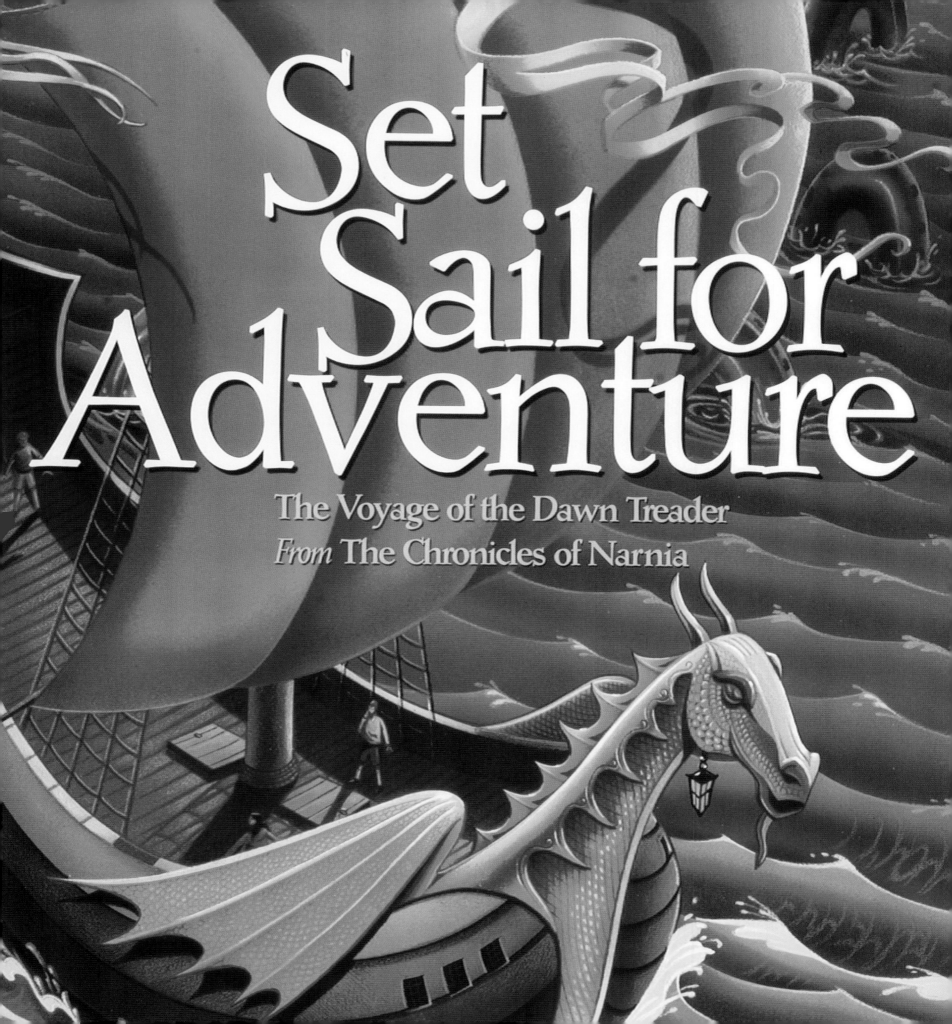

Set Sail for Adventure

The Voyage of the Dawn Treader

From The Chronicles of Narnia

RADIO THEATRE

RECOGNIZING THE SUCCESS OF *ADVENTURES IN ODYSSEY,* Focus asked the question: Could top-quality radio drama experience a revival among adults as well as children? Given our TV- and video-laden society, Focus believed families would choose to sit and listen, letting their imaginations supply the visual imagery instead of being force-fed special effects and light shows.

Longtime *AIO* writer and executive producer Paul McCusker recalls, "Back in 1992, Dave Arnold, then our production manager, and I began brainstorming how we could take audio drama a step beyond *Adventures in Odyssey.* We toyed with several ideas, including a new drama series based on one idea or, better yet, an anthology program such as *Masterpiece Theatre* or *Mystery!* that would tell different kinds of stories from week to week."

As time went on, Paul and Dave changed and refined the original idea, and they became more passionate about using dramas to reach those who didn't know Christ.

"Our motivation was to spread God's truth the same way Jesus did: through story-telling," Dave Arnold recalls. "We wanted to present stories with a solid Christian worldview but without the kinds of obvious words and phrases that would instantly alienate those who aren't Christians. We became convinced that we must only use the best stories and bring a new level of sound production to the process. We knew we'd need to record with different actors, to present a new style of acting. This led us to London, England. It was cost effective to record there, which opened the door for us to work with world-renowned actors such as Paul Scofield, David Suchet, Ron Moody, and Joan Plowright."

The series was dubbed *Focus on the Family Radio Theatre,* and the first production was the Dickens classic *A Christmas Carol.* The writers and producers were determined to create a "definitive version" of the tale that not only stayed true to Dickens's original book, but would also be recorded with top British actors. The dedication to high standards paid off: The Focus production of *A Christmas Carol* premiered in 1996 on more secular and Christian radio stations than any other radio special in history. It has since become a regular holiday feature on many stations across the nation.

David Suchet, top, the voice of Aslan in our *Chronicles of Narnia* series, is well known to TV viewers as Hercule Poirot in the long-running *Agatha Christie* mysteries.

Dame Joan Plowright, above, is the storyteller in *The Secret Garden,* and one of Britain's leading actresses.

A recording session for *Bonhoeffer: The Cost of Freedom* in England.

Opposite: A poster advertising C. S. Lewis's "The Voyage of the Dawn Treader," fifth in the *Chronicles of Narnia* series.

The team then followed up with a production on the life of Dietrich Bonhoeffer. "Whether you agree or disagree with Bonhoeffer's theology, few can deny that his story makes for compelling drama," says McCusker. "Again, we pulled out all the stops in the writing, acting, and sound design."

The production of *Bonhoeffer: The Cost of Freedom* was awarded the prestigious Peabody Award in 1998, competing with both secular and religious productions. Since then, our *Radio Theatre* team has produced original dramas of *The Father Gilbert Mysteries* and *The Luke Reports,* alongside such classics as *Les Misérables, Silas Marner, The Secret Garden,* and *Ben Hur.*

The most ambitious project the team undertook has been the adaptation of C. S. Lewis's beloved *Chronicles of Narnia,* a seven-part fantasy allegory. Despite production challenges and sky-high expectations, the series has been an unqualified hit. In fact, National Public Radio aired the initial installment, "The Lion, the Witch and the Wardrobe"—the first time any Focus radio program has penetrated that market.

"God continues to get His message into the hands—and ears—of people around the world through Focus's radio dramas," Dave Arnold says. "Many people who would never read the Bible or attend church will listen to a compelling, well-told story on the radio. It's humbling and exciting to be a part of His plan in this way." ■

Brian Blessed, top, the voice of Jean Valjean in the *Radio Theatre* production of *Les Misérables*, was the voice of Boss Nass in Disney's *Tarzan*.

Paul Scofield, above, the storyteller in our *Chronicles of Narnia* series, won an Academy Award for his performance in *A Man for All Seasons*.

Dave Arnold, producer of *Radio Theatre*, accepts the prestigious Peabody Award for *Bonhoeffer: The Cost of Freedom*, above. The award is pictured at left with other *Radio Theatre* albums.

Actors and staff enjoy a relaxed moment during a *Radio Theatre* recording session in London, at right.

LIFE ON THE EDGE—LIVE!

SINCE TEENS IN OUR SOCIETY are bombarded with bad advice and degrading images, where can they turn for positive, healthy, and godly input? One place is a Focus broadcast called *Life on the Edge~Live!*, which features a live question-and-answer format on Saturday nights that allows callers to ask about anything and everything.

The idea for a teen broadcast germinated over many years, and along the way, several test programs were created and evaluated. Of those early demo shows, none clicked. Then, in 1997, Focus found a winning combination when teen expert Joe White and *Brio* magazine editor Susie Shellenberger got together before the microphones. Responding to teens' queries, the hosts offer sound biblical advice on topics ranging from school problems to sexuality, from dating to drugs. Many teens have said they appreciate the practical answers to tough, real-life issues.

Jeff Caylor, producer of *Life on the Edge~Live!*, recalls the night in April 2000 when a boy called in and told Joe White he didn't believe the Bible's account of Jesus' life. Joe presented some convincing evidence:

"The call ended and we thought it was just another seed planted that would never come to fruition," Jeff remembers. "The following week, our screener took a call from the same teen. This time he called to thank us for our show. A friend who had heard him on the radio the week before brought up the subject after school one day. As a result, he ended up praying with his friend to accept Christ right there on the soccer field."

Score another victory for truth. ∎

Co-hosts Susie Shellenberger and Joe White, pictured above on a promotional poster, take calls each week on teen-related topics. (Steve Russo replaced Joe in 2002.)

Teens today are under a lot of pressure. *Life on the Edge—Live!* is one place they can go for answers.

Life on the Edge—Live! was awarded Talk Show of the Year by the National Religious Broadcasters Association in February 2000, as seen at left.

"To do a broadcast under the banner of Focus on the Family is like making a cup of homemade soup and calling it 'Campbell's.' The trust, the admiration, and the respect for the Focus on the Family name across America is like no other family ministry name in the world. Dr. Dobson helped raise my kids and now it is my privilege to come alongside him and help raise America's kids. It has been one of the greatest joys of my lifetime." —JOE WHITE, PRESIDENT OF KANAKUK KAMPS AND FORMER CO-HOST OF *LIFE ON THE EDGE—LIVE!*

RENEWING THE HEART

WOMEN TODAY OCCUPY KEY ROLES in many aspects of society—businesses, corporations, churches, government, and, of course, families. And while many women feel grateful for the opportunity to fulfill their potential and utilize their God-given talents, others feel inferior or "second class" if they choose to become wives and mothers. What a tragic perception!

To address this and many other issues women face, Focus began Renewing the Heart Women's Ministries in 1997. This outreach provides support, encouragement, and advice to women in all walks of life. Most importantly, we try to affirm the unique calling God has for Christian women—whether they be stay-at-home moms or corporate executives.

A centerpiece of this ministry is a weekly call-in broadcast each Saturday afternoon hosted by Janet Parshall. This program provides a forum for women to discuss concerns and receive biblical advice. The call-in format always delivers lively discussion, as Janet and her guests answer questions from callers live on air, addressing everything from money management to family issues. "Sitting behind the microphone as host of *Renewing the Heart*," says Janet, "I have come to hear the heart cry of women who hunger for God. They desire to know that He loves them. They seek His healing for their wounded hearts, and they long to live as women after God's own heart. Our desire is to bring women back to the Word of life, the Bible, and to remind them weekly that in Christ Jesus, their hearts will be renewed." ∎

Truth and Grace for Daily Living

Our Women's Ministries department offers opportunities for mentoring as well as renewal.

Opposite: *Renewing the Heart* host Janet Parshall (right) interviews guest Terry Willits before taking calls during one of the broadcasts.

GOD IS IN THE DETAILS

As a producer of the *Renewing the Heart* call-in show, Wendy Selvig has seen tremendous growth in the women's ministry. God's hand has been present in every aspect of the show—especially in the details. She recounts one such incident:

"One Thursday, before the broadcast, I had a strong urge to call Janet and ask her to tape a generic ending for the show—just in case we ever lost the ISDN connection with her, which would be horribly inconclusive and unprofessional. I could tell from her voice that she thought the request a little strange, but she complied and sent me a pretaped ending. I had it ready to go that Saturday, and wouldn't you know it: We got to the end of the show and the ISDN flaked out and dropped. We lost Janet! Gratefully, I reached over to the mini-disk, hit play, and the generic ending came on. No one could tell that she wasn't there with us. This had never happened before, and has never happened since. Praise God for His leading and guidance—with His help, we will stay on the air!"

PART THREE

MINISTRY WITH A PERSONAL TOUCH

A Commitment to Compassionate Outreach

"Dear friends, let us love one another, for love comes from God."

[1 John 4:7]

They're just like part of our family.... I feel like I know Dr. Dobson.... Focus has become an extended family to me...." We consistently hear comments like these from people who listen to *Focus on the Family* on a regular basis. They feel a kinship and familiarity with Dr. and Mrs. Dobson, as well as with our frequent guests on the broadcast. Indeed, Dr. Dobson's communication style on the radio (and in his books and newsletters) has often been described as folksy and unpretentious, as if he were saying, "Let's sit down over a cup of coffee and chat about this issue." This kind of warm, friendly relationship gives people the feeling that they can just pick up the phone to call us or sit down to jot us a note. And we're delighted our friends feel such freedom!

In the early years, a handful of staff responded to the calls and letters that came in from our listeners asking questions and requesting advice. As the ministry grew, it became a challenge to maintain that sense of personal connection with our audience.

The volume of mail and calls has grown rapidly as broadcast distribution increased, new ministry efforts were launched, and the kinds of needs we address have become more complex as the culture around us changed. Currently, almost one-third of our employees are directly involved in communicating with those who contact us by letter, phone, or e-mail.

For those who are able to pay a personal visit to our campus, our Guest Relations staff loves to extend a warm welcome. They have had the opportunity to laugh with many families, cry with others, and offer encouragement and support. It's a privilege to share with our guests the great things God is accomplishing here, and we love hearing what He is doing in their own families. Such dialogue has been an important part of Focus on the Family since it first began, and it will continue to be as long as we exist.

Every year, Focus on the Family's Correspondence department staff responds, promptly and personally, to thousands of letters, e-mails, and phone calls—all dealing with a broad range of topics.

KEEPING IN TOUCH

It began as a trickle . . . which grew into a stream . . . and eventually became a full-fledged flood.

The "flood" in question is the volume of mail received by Focus—the thousands of cards and letters that arrive each day bearing questions, inquiries, and requests for help. Make no mistake: Focus considers this flood to be a great blessing, offering us the opportunity to participate in God's ministry to people around the world.

In the first few months of the new ministry, Dr. Dobson, with the help of a secretary, struggled to respond to each letter as it came in. It wasn't long, however, before the volume reached a point at which he needed help—lots of help—with the enormous task of keeping up this personal side of Focus on the Family's outreach. That's how our Correspondence department was born.

This behind-the-scenes aspect of our ministry had a humble beginning. It started with one or two staff members being hired each time the mail volume increased. They shared a tiny office in the Arcadia, California, headquarters. By 1987, the Correspondence staff had grown to about forty people and had been moved to rented office space a few blocks from our other buildings on East Foothill Boulevard in Arcadia. From there to Pomona, and from Pomona to Colorado Springs, as the flow of incoming mail increased, the ministry moved to accommodate more staff to handle more requests.

We begin every workday with a devotional time, praying for each other as well as for the specific needs of those who contact the ministry for help.

The Correspondence team now comprises one of Focus's largest departments, numbering more than one hundred members. The handful of letters that came to us during our early years has grown to more than thirty-six thousand per week. Naturally, it's difficult to maintain a personal touch while responding to such a huge volume of mail. But this is the mission to which the Correspondence staff has committed itself: Within the context of our large, mass-media ministry, we strive to create personal relationships with the thousands of people who take the time to write us.

As we see it, every individual who contacts us is important to God—far too important to be dismissed with an impersonal form letter. We respond to each letter, whether it comes from a desperate parent, a troubled teen, or an eight-year-old child with a question about a recent episode of *Adventures in Odyssey*. What's more, the Correspondence team conducts careful research on a variety of issues in order to provide consistent, current, and accurate advice when questions come to us.

This story wouldn't be complete, of course, without prayer. Many of the letters specifically request prayer for serious family needs or concerns. Sometimes the best thing we can say in response to a letter—sometimes the *only* thing—is that we will pray. And we do. The Focus staff considers it a privilege to bring each request, by name, before the Lord. One of the greatest blessings we receive is the thrill of hearing back from families who have seen and experienced God's answers to our prayers. What an honor it is to serve in this way! ■

TRIUMPH OVER TRAGEDY

Tour groups stop along "Main Street" to learn more about the ministry.

ONE WOMAN AND HER SON joined forty other people on a tour of our facilities. When they arrived in the area overlooking the Correspondence department, she asked if she could share a personal story with the group.

A few years before, she said, her husband had committed suicide. The couple's ten-year-old son had been the one who discovered his father. The grieving and distraught widow had no family or close friends to help her through her grief. Although she was not a Christian, she had heard of "some organization that was called Focus on the Family" and decided to write a letter asking for any support and advice we could provide.

When Focus received the letter, a Correspondence assistant sent back an encouraging note and also forwarded the woman's information to a counselor. The counselor called her and spoke with her for an hour. Focus also sent two boxes. The one addressed to the mother included a Bible, several booklets related to her situation, and a copy of Dr. Dobson's book *When God Doesn't Make Sense.* Her son received a box containing a children's Bible, a couple of *McGee and Me* videos, some *Adventures in Odyssey* audiotapes, and several children's books.

The boy began to read his Bible, watch the videos, and listen to the tapes. God spoke to him and, on his own, he prayed to receive Christ as his Savior. Then he went to tell his mother what he had done, adding, "Mommy, you need Jesus." She, too, sank to her knees and accepted Christ.

For more than two years, this mother and son scrimped and saved until they could afford to take a trip from Michigan. Their plan for the perfect vacation? A visit to Colorado Springs to express their thanks to Focus on the Family for caring for them in their most difficult moments and for bringing them into God's Kingdom. ∎

Opposite: Guest Relations staff person Diane Ingolia talks to a group of visitors about Focus's various radio programs, and shows maps that indicate where the broadcasts are aired.

Focus resources, at right, are often sent to assist and encourage families seeking help.

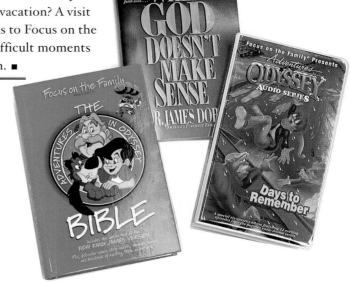

THE GIFT OF SACRIFICE

FOCUS ON THE FAMILY RECOGNIZES that our ministry is dependent on the giving of God's people. We strongly urge people to give first to their local church and then to support para-church organizations such as Focus on the Family above that primary obligation if they are able. We understand that for many, the dollars that they donate to ministries like Focus come at great sacrifice.

Nearly a decade ago, one family—the Thompsons—reinforced this understanding in a letter that has become a part of Focus history:

> Please find enclosed a check for $17. When we received your letter last month concerning your financial difficulties, we talked about it in our family. The children were quite willing to send you some of their own money from their allowances—but we did not want them to do something like that because it seemed too easy. So, we talked to them about the idea of sacrifice—what it means to give up something for someone else. This may sound silly, but we decided to give up boxed cereals, store-bought bread, and candy for one week.
>
> This may seem very small, but especially to our four-year-old, it was major! So much so that she would hardly eat anything the first morning of the week—and she normally eats right away! But we drew up a calendar for her, and the rest of the week went well. The children also made cookies and brought them to church. They just had a sign up saying the cookies were free, but anyone who wished to donate to Focus could do so. So, the total amount they came up with is $17. We are thankful that you were honest in saying you were in financial need—it has given our family the opportunity to talk about things we may not normally talk about. We're glad we could help out in this small way.

When Dr. Dobson received this letter, he duplicated it for the entire staff with this comment: "I believe there are thousands of families like these precious people who do without things they need so that we might have the funds to operate this ministry. This is what I call 'blood money.' We are morally obligated to use every dollar conservatively and wisely! Waste and extravagance must not be tolerated.

"The only way to eliminate waste and extravagance is for every [employee] to be careful with the resources God has given. That's why I'm asking each of you to keep the Thompson comment in mind as you travel, as you use the Xerox machine, as you make telephone calls, as you request computers and staples and furniture." ∎

Our Correspondence staff in California, pictured in the 1980s, responds to letters from constituents.

Opposite: Our Distribution Center staff, circa 1987, packages books, tapes, and videos requested by ministry friends.

"Fully a hundred times over the past fifteen years, I've had someone come up to me at a seminar and say, 'You know Dr. Dobson, don't you?' It's my honor to say yes, and then to listen to the story of another changed life from a radio broadcast, a book, or even a letter from Focus on the Family." —DR. JOHN TRENT, PRESIDENT OF STRONGFAMILIES.COM

ANSWERING THE CALL

FROM THE VERY BEGINNING, Focus has placed a high priority on ministering with a personal touch. Dr. Dobson and the Focus leadership continually remind the staff that every letter, every phone call, every e-mail message is vitally important and should be handled with great care. In essence, we attempt to be a high-touch ministry in a low-touch world.

This attitude is evident every day in our Constituent Response division. The goal of this team, which consists of more than 250 employees, is to respond quickly and sensitively to the needs and requests of people who contact Focus via the phone or mail. Letters are sent through to our Correspondence or Counseling departments, and requests for materials are forwarded to our Distribution Center.

Calls coming into the Correspondence and Constituent Response departments, above and below, are handled by real people who care about the callers and are there to help.

When someone phones the ministry, the call is answered by a live voice. Callers are not met by a recording or sent through a labyrinthine phone menu system. (The only exception is when our phone staff is overloaded and callers are placed on hold.) We fully realize that how we treat people is a testimony to the gracious, caring God we serve. One family wrote a note following a phone conversation with a Constituent Response team member:

> Our son was killed in a car accident on Easter Sunday. Friends and even our pastor had turned away from us, not knowing how to respond to parents who had lost a child. I called to find out about materials that could help my wife and me through the grieving process. Along with the requested resource list, we received a package of tapes and books, including *When God Doesn't Make Sense*. We had believed that no one knew how to reach out to us, but you were there when all the others turned their backs. You did more than provide materials; you gave us a hug at a critical moment.

Letters such as this are deeply meaningful to us. They assure us that we are fulfilling our mission to supply—in a practical way—the hope and healing that comes from God Himself. ■

Our Constituent Response staff, at right, discusses options for handling an increased number of calls and letters coming in response to a broadcast. This photo was taken at 50 East Foothill in Arcadia, California, around 1987.

"I had written a letter to Focus on the Family when my marriage was falling apart. I didn't know what to do and I asked for help—any help. I didn't really expect anything from the letter but I sent it anyway. I could not believe it when about one week later I received a phone call from a Focus on the Family employee who wanted to know how things were going and whether I was doing okay. By then that particular crisis had passed, but it was a real turning point for me. It made me realize that I was not alone. That there are people out there, willing and able to help if I only seek the help I need." —DIEGO MERA, CONSTITUENT

ENCOURAGING WORDS

STAFF MEMBERS IN OUR CONSTITUENT RESPONSE DEPARTMENT never know what issue they'll confront when they pick up the phone. Most often, the calls are simple and straightforward: "Can you please send me a copy of the latest video?" Others are more sensitive and heartrending.

Cathy Wahlstrom remembers a poignant call she handled: "A dad phoned to say he needed advice and help. He had come home from work that day for lunch, picked up the mail, and started looking through it. He opened his credit card bill and tossed the other letters on the kitchen table. Listed on the bill were charges he hadn't made."

When the man called the credit card company to complain, he was told that he had authorized the charges. After further investigation, he was jolted by an even bigger surprise: the purchases were for pornographic videos.

He knew then that only one person could have ordered those items—his teenage son. He ran upstairs to the boy's room, searching for the evidence. When he found the videos, he discovered they were not only pornographic, but also homosexual in nature. Furious and hurt, he took the videos downstairs and slammed them on the table. Pondering how he should respond, he sank into a kitchen chair with his head bowed.

"Right below him on the table, in the stack of letters, was a mailer from Focus on the Family," Cathy continues. "He picked up the phone and called—and that's when I answered. I assured him we would be able to help him. He started to give me his name and then broke down crying. I just waited, telling him to go ahead and cry and to take as long as he needed. After five minutes, he regained his composure enough to give me his information."

Later, the man called Cathy's supervisor to say thank you. He had been given the name of a Christian counselor in his area. He had picked his son up from school and driven straight to a counseling appointment, which had been a tremendous help. He was also sent Focus materials to provide information and assistance.

"This man said that if he hadn't seen that flyer from us and called, he's not sure how he would have reacted to his son," Cathy says. "I am continually amazed how God directs people to Focus at just the right time so we can provide the help and encouragement they need." ■

Members of our Pomona Correspondence team in the late 1980s, opposite. Before our system was computerized, the staff referred to hundreds of pages of Focus research when responding to constituents. Today the phone systems and research are computerized, but the response is still personal.

"For the last eighteen years I have had the privilege of serving God on the board of Focus on the Family. My walk with Christ has been accelerated as I've watched Him direct and use Jim, Shirley, and the dedicated staff there. These people walk their talk, and we look forward to watching God use them through Focus on the Family for many years to come." —LEE EATON, PRESIDENT OF EATON FARMS INC. AND FOCUS ON THE FAMILY BOARD MEMBER

WHAT HAPPENS TO ALL THOSE LETTERS?

Most phone calls and letters are sent first through Constituent Response, pictured above in Pomona in the late 1980s.

A member of the production staff, opposite, selects items requested by a constituent and loads them into the coded container that holds that person's order. It will then pass down the line until it reaches the packing and shipping area.

WHEN SOMEONE WRITES A LETTER to Focus, what happens to it? Most people understand that it would be humanly impossible for Dr. Dobson to read the thousands of letters that arrive here each day. Nevertheless, each piece of mail is given careful handling and a personal reply.

Staff members in our Operations Building carefully review every letter and forward it to the proper department or individual for response. Donations to the ministry or requests for resources are handled in the Constituent Response department. Letters asking for advice or assistance move to the Correspondence department, where individual replies are crafted based on Dr. Dobson's writings and statements. Other letters refer to publications, broadcasts, or public policy action steps, and they are sent to the appropriate department. Letters that include prayer requests are distributed among staff members, who pray over each one. Dr. Dobson is then sent a summary of the mail and the comments made by our friends for the past month.

In 2001, new technology was implemented that allows a piece of mail to be digitally scanned and delivered to several recipients at the same time. That's important, since we receive an average of thirty-six thousand letters each week and many of them express multiple requests—from prayer to the desire for a book to the need for parental advice. We are determined not to drop any of these requests, which may be critical to the person who sent them. ■

At top, thousands of our resources are printed, sorted, inventoried, and then picked from the shelves as requests come in.

Each letter is opened and read by a trained staff member, above, who does his or her best to meet the needs of the constituent.

"I was a single mom, working part time, in school full time, and looking for badly needed sources of encouragement. I saw a booklet list from Focus, but as I made my way down the list, I found myself putting a check mark by almost every one. When I figured out the cost, I had exceeded my budget, so I got out my eraser and applied some self-control. When I received the package, I found every one of the booklets I'd originally checked! Some sharp eyes had detected my erasures, assessed my situation, and decided to send some unconditional love my way." —ANONYMOUS CONSTITUENT

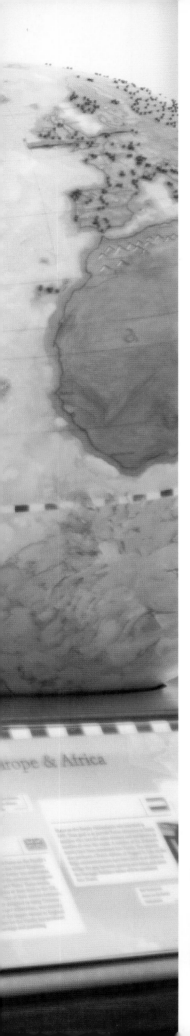

BE OUR GUEST

EACH YEAR, FOCUS ON THE FAMILY WELCOMES more than 200,000 visitors. That is a huge number of people! Where do these folks come from, and why do they visit our campus?

During a typical month, we see guests from forty-eight different states and twenty countries. Our visitors might be enthusiastic young fans of *Adventures in Odyssey,* or they might have booked our birthday party room for a celebration. Our guests come from retirement homes, day camps, churches, and home school groups. They are truck drivers, foreign pastors, physicians, and college students. They might be paying a visit to Focus on their honeymoon or their fiftieth-wedding-anniversary trip.

They come because Dr. Dobson and Focus's ministry have touched their lives in a personal way. We've heard many people comment, "Coming here is like coming home." That's because they feel like they know Dr. Dobson after hearing his warm voice on the radio countless times…or because they were helped by a Focus counselor at a critical time…or because our resources got them through a tough child-rearing period…or because they received an encouraging word when they called.

Whoever they are and wherever they're from, our guests want to tell their personal stories—and we love to hear them! It touches our hearts to hear about marriages that are mended because of Dr. Dobson's book *Love Must Be Tough.* We've met and hugged the children who were saved because of our materials on the sanctity of human life. We've cried with the parents who have lost their children to cancer or leukemia. And we rejoiced with the truck driver who received Christ after hearing *Adventures in Odyssey.*

One day, an elderly gentleman rushed in to our Welcome Center, knowing he would find refuge there. He was running away from home, where his adult daughter had been beating him. We fed him, counseled him, called the proper authorities, and prayed for him.

Another father drove from Kansas. He had just lost his son to AIDS and then his wife of fifty-three years to cancer. He came to Focus knowing he'd see families that, as he said, "will bring me great comfort." We hugged him, cried with him, and loved him. He stayed all day.

A young mom was playing with her adopted toddler in Kid's Korner. The little Russian girl was paralyzed from the waist down due to a failed abortion. They came because Focus had given the direction and counsel the mother needed to make the adoption from Russia possible. We rejoiced with her.

These are just a few of the hundreds of heartwarming—and sometimes heart-wrenching—stories we hear each year. We count it a blessing to participate in God's work in the lives of people such as these. ∎

Guests can enjoy the many entertaining areas of the Welcome Center—designed just for kids!

Opposite: Visitors to the Focus on the Family Welcome Center can use many interactive displays to learn about the ministry's efforts both in the United States and around the world.

At far left, a group of young guests dress up and perform on stage on the lower level of the Welcome Center. Another group, near left, views the gallery of artwork by James Dobson Sr., located on the main floor.

THE WELCOME MAT IS ALWAYS OUT

VISITORS TO FOCUS ENJOY THE OPPORTUNITY to tour our facilities and get an up-close-and-personal view of how our ministry operates. In the Welcome Center, displays help guests learn about our radio broadcasts, films, periodicals, and other outreach efforts. This building also features two art galleries, a specialty coffee bar, and a theater that shows a video about the history and purpose of Focus called *Coming Home*.

The Guest Relations hosts conduct tours of the Administration Building that include the central corridor (dubbed "Main Street" by staff), with its maps pinpointing broadcast locations and awards presented to books, films, and periodicals; the Correspondence area, where department staff answer all the mail; the broadcast studio, where Dr. Dobson and his guests record programs; and the combination chapel and cafeteria, known as the "Chapelteria." Some visitors choose to see the Operations Building, which may be the most interesting place of all.

A couple from New Zealand visited Focus one day and told a Guest Relations host about the grief caused by their fifteen-year-old daughter years before. She had gone through a rebellious stage that included drug use and an out-of-wedlock pregnancy. Her distraught and angry father didn't want to face the situation, so he planned to run away. He was going to take a plane to the farthest place he could think of—Alaska!

Jumping into his car, he had sped toward the airport with the radio on—which just happened to be playing the *Focus* broadcast. The program that day was "Dad, I'm Pregnant." The man said he'd never stopped to think about how his daughter was feeling, and he'd turned around and gone home, ready to reach out to her. Now, visiting Focus, he gave God complete credit for His perfect timing. And then he began to tell the host all about his beautiful four-year-old granddaughter.

Two other international guests—students from Romania—took a tour, and one of them, Alex, told the hostess he and his church had been praying for America because they heard it was "very bad here." The other student, Adina, remarked how sad it was that this country had abandoned its Christian heritage.

Adina went on to say they had been in the United States for two weeks and had not seen evidence of devotion to God anywhere in the entire country. However, at the conclusion of the tour, she said with tears in her eyes, "Today, here in this place, we have found Him! Never have we seen such freedom."

No one could give us a better compliment. ∎

Dr. Dobson and Mike Trout welcome the Weber family, above left. One of the Webers was the one-millionth visitor to our Colorado campus on April 25, 2000.

Families browse through our bookstore, shown opposite. Remodeled in 2000, it features all Focus on the Family titles as well as Dr. Dobson's books. It also sells many of the other family resources offered by the ministry.

Below, *The Gazette*, Colorado Springs's local newspaper, features an article about Focus on the Family's popularity as a local tourist attraction.

Focus on Family joins list of area's top tourist draws

New attractions aimed at bringing in youngsters

By **Dave Curtin**
The Gazette

Focus on the Family is the seventh most popular tourist attraction in the Pikes Peak region. Its 200,000 annual visitors rank it just behind the Cheyenne Mountain Zoo and just ahead of the U.S. Olympic Complex.

but some day these youngsters will be old enough to receive the word of God, and that's the bottom line. We're providing a positive Christian experience for them," says Ken Roth, manager of guest relations at Focus on the Family, a nonprofit ministry dedicated to the preservation of the home.

The ministry, located on a 77-acre campus in the Briargate

IF YOU GO

Focus on the Family is at 8605 Explorer Drive. Take the Briargate exit off Interstate 25.
The Welcome Center and Kids' Korner is open 9 a.m.-5 p.m. Monday-Saturday.
Whit's End Soda Shoppe, is open 10 a.m.-4 p.m., Monday-Saturday.

THE WELCOME CENTER

The front of the Focus on the Family Welcome Center, with Pikes Peak in the background.

The back of the building features a three-story slide.

Visitors enjoy the interactive broadcast outreach area.

Dr. and Shirley Dobson participate in the dedication chapel for the new Welcome Center on September 16, 1994.

Ed and Elsa Prince proposed and funded the Welcome Center for the ministry.

Kids get a good laugh as Dr. Dobson tries out the new slide.

The kids' area downstairs includes a story corner, where guests can read to their children.

Children have fun and burn up some energy in the play area.

Families can have lunch or snacks at Whit's End six days a week.

Youngsters perform on a stage complete with lights and costumes.

Last Chance Detectives fans can visit a B-17 just like the one in the videos!

Kids enjoy videos in the Adventures in Odyssey theater.

HEY, THAT'S NOT A BAD IDEA!

Apparently, Dr. Dobson's reputation as a child-rearing expert doesn't guarantee that children will behave while visiting Focus. After all, we've seen our share of temper tantrums and outbursts of sibling rivalry during guest tours.

One family was taking a tour, and the parents were having a tough time keeping their rambunctious seven-year-old boy under control. As the mother marched her son toward the restroom, she passed the front desk.

Gripping the boy's arm tightly, she stopped just long enough to declare to the Guest Relations person at the desk, "You need a Dare to Discipline Room!"

KIDS WILL BE KIDS!

DR. DOBSON HAS ALWAYS HAD GREAT AFFECTION TOWARD CHILDREN and both he and the staff consider it a great privilege to meet the thousands of little tykes who, with their parents, visit our campus each year. Here are a few gems "from the mouths of babes" we've heard over the years:

One mom told us about the time her toddler had disobeyed her. The mother told the little girl she would have to spank her for her disobedience, but the child responded, "No, Mom, you can't spank me now." When the mother asked why not, the little one replied, "Because you're going to have to check with Dr. Dobson first."

In the hallways near our Correspondence department, many of Dr. Dobson's academic robes and collars are displayed, recognizing the numerous honorary degrees he has been awarded by various universities. Stopping in front of the display, a little boy asked a tour guide if Dr. Dobson was a messy eater. "I don't think so," she replied, "but why do you ask?" "He must be," the boy said. "Just look at all those bibs!"

On a tour with a group of children, the guide asked how many of the kids knew who Dr. Dobson is. "I know him!" one little boy excitedly said. "My mom reads *Cat in the Hat* to me every night!" Wrong doctor, apparently.

One day, two brothers visited Focus headquarters and were looking at a black-and-white picture of Dr. Dobson from the 1970s (his long-sideburn era). The nine-year-old asked, "Who do you think that is?" His eleven-year-old brother offered a guess: "I think it's Dr. Blackgaard from *Adventures in Odyssey*." "Nah," the younger one replied. "I think it's that Dr. Kangaroo guy."

A father told us about the time he was getting dressed while his two little girls were in his room. He was attempting to be discreet because of their presence, and one asked why he was acting different. "I'm trying to be modest," the dad told them. The younger one replied, "It's okay, Daddy! We listen to *Adventures in Modesty* all the time."

One ten-year-old girl wrote this letter to the ministry: "Dear Mr. Dr. Dobson: My pappa always says that momma and him raised me by your rules (for me and them). I know if I have kids I will raise mine the same way—your way. I know that if they didn't have you I would probably be a brat." ∎

At top, two girls act out story roles in the stage area of the Welcome Center.

Three young visitors, above middle, peruse Focus resources in the *Clubhouse* area of the bookstore in Pomona, California.

Dr. Dobson holds Katie Will, above, granddaughter of the Bingamans, longtime Focus friends.

Opposite: Proud dad Dr. Dobson shows his daughter's Woof series to a group of children in his office.

"Focus on the Family has helped me to stand strong in the decision I made three years ago to become a stay-at-home mommy. Sometimes, when you're up to your neck in dirty diapers and kiddie videos, it's nice to be reminded that 'If anyone wants to be first, he must be the very last, and the servant of all.' When my three-year-old shows people my Bible and says, 'My mommy loves Jesus,' I know I made the right decision! Thank you, Dr. Dobson, for being my lifeline!" —ANGIE CARVER, CONSTITUENT

A Special Guest Star

Elaine Nelson leads a tour group through the halls of Focus in Pomona, California, giving information and answering questions along the way.

THE TEAM IN OUR GUEST RELATIONS DEPARTMENT—which greets visitors, answers questions, and provides tours at our headquarters—have countless stories of how the Lord has orchestrated "coincidences" with folks who walk through our doors. Elaine Nelson, the first Guest Relations representative for Focus, tells the story of one such God-ordained encounter:

While Focus was still located in Pomona, a couple with a young girl rushed into the lobby after normal business hours, around 5:45 P.M. It was obvious they had pushed hard to make it before closing. The couple explained that they were from Kansas and that day was their daughter's eleventh birthday. For months she had looked forward to seeing the *Adventures in Odyssey* studio and meeting the cast. Their visit to California and Focus was the fulfillment of her birthday wish.

I swallowed hard, knowing the studio was almost certainly empty since most of the staff had left for the day. I promised to take them on a tour of the Broadcast department, but I prepared the girl, Kim, for disappointment. As I escorted them up the stairs leading to the studio, Kim became very talkative and animated. She was vivacious and obviously quite bright. At the studio's viewing window, I excused myself and entered the separate recording room around the back. Two of the *AIO* producers were working feverishly and looking exasperated.

Sheepishly, I ventured, "I'm sorry to barge in like this, guys, but you have to do me a favor and talk to a girl whose birthday happiness hinges on this…"

Their eyes got big, and they practically jumped out of their seats.

"Can she act?" one of them nearly shouted. It sounded like a plea of desperation.

When I looked puzzled, the other guy said, "We spent all day auditioning kids for a special segment of *Adventures in Odyssey* and have hit a brick wall. We've got to have it ready tomorrow!"

"Well, she seems pretty precocious," I said.

"Bring her in."

Grinning from ear to ear, I invited the family into the studio. Kim was ushered to a stool and a script was shoved into one hand and a mike in the other.

"Kim, would you like to make believe you're reading a script for a broadcast? Just pretend you are acting in your own room and don't think about us."

As Kim began reading, we were mesmerized. Her tone, pacing, and inflection were flawless. Within half an hour, the lines had been polished and recorded to perfection. The broadcast would be ready for airing as planned, and a young girl and her parents were elated beyond words.

All I could say was, "Thank You, God, for caring about the little things in life!" ■

Visitors to the *Adventures in Odyssey* area of the Welcome Center can record their own voices in a real *AIO* episode and then take a tape of the program home with them.

IN PRAISE OF PASTORS

Focus on the Family takes seriously Paul's words to the Thessalonians, "Now we ask you, brothers, to respect those who work hard among you, who are over you in the Lord and who admonish you. Hold them in the highest regard in love because of their work" (1 Thessalonians 5:12-13). As a result, Focus's Ministry Outreach department was actively involved in designating October as Clergy Appreciation Month in 1994. The aim is to encourage churches and denominations to express appreciation to ministers and their families.

The Ministry Outreach team has created a packet of suggestions for congregations to use in planning this event. The message is getting out—Focus constituents have requested more than twenty thousand Clergy Appreciation Month kits annually for the past several years.

MINISTERING TO THE MINISTERS

FROM ITS INCEPTION, FOCUS HAS BEEN ADAMANT that our ministry support and assist local churches in every way possible. Through the years, Dr. Dobson has repeatedly urged people to give financial support to churches first, and only then to consider contributing to Focus. "The local church is the first line of defense for families. We are secondary in that effort."

In 1991, Focus formalized its support of churches when we launched our Ministry Outreach department, spearheaded by H. B. London Jr., who was a pastor for thirty years before joining our organization. The primary effort of this division involves caring for ministry families. As H. B. and his team know well, pastors live in a world of constant demands, of being stretched and criticized, of living under a magnifying glass.

Clergy members and their spouses know that they will receive encouragement and a listening ear when they call the Pastoral Care Hotline at Focus. In some cases, the callers just need a booster shot of understanding; in others, more serious counseling care is needed. Regional gatherings are also held so that pastoral families can meet together for fellowship and inspiration. Pastoral outreach luncheons have even been provided overseas.

The Ministry Outreach team also coordinates the planning and production of our monthly chapels and oversees physician outreach efforts to connect with medical professionals. In addition, the Youth Culture department—which produces the newsletter *Plugged In* and many other resources for parents of teens and youth pastors—is under the guidance of Ministry Outreach.

Many people know that H. B. London is Dr. Dobson's cousin, but few know how the two came to work together at Focus. H. B. provides some background:

> I'm an only child, as is Jim Dobson. As my first cousin, he is the closest thing I have to a brother. Since we both grew up in pastors' homes, we learned very early the challenges faced by those in ministry. In 1985, through God's providence, I became the Dobsons' pastor. It was during our time in Pasadena, California, that we began to discuss the burden on clergy families. We talked openly about how much of the crisis mail and phone calls received at Focus came from pastors.
>
> We began to explore the possibility of our working together. The chance of that being successful appeared pretty remote, but as time went on the subject would resurface. One day we said, "If it's okay with Beverley and Shirley, and God doesn't stop us, let's give it a try." And we did.
>
> In November 1991, I resigned my pastorate in Southern California and moved immediately to Colorado Springs to begin my assignment as a pastor to pastors. It has been one of the most rewarding and challenging assignments of my professional life. Since then I've spoken in more than eighty denominations and have worked with hundreds of thousands of pastors. I thank God for the opportunity to serve in this great cause. ∎

Pastoral Ministries has been holding Pastors' Gatherings across the country since 1992. More than forty thousand pastors and spouses have attended.

At top, H. B. and Beverley London pose with Jim and Shirley Dobson. Above, Jim and H. B. in college.

Opposite: Attendees pray together at one of the pastors' conferences held at Focus's Colorado headquarters.

"I called your hotline to talk about my feelings of failure as a pastor and father. I'd wanted to throw in the towel and resign although I have five children and no other source of income. The Christlike brother who spoke with me calmed me down and helped me regain my perspective. He prayed with me and gave me wise counsel. I could sense his prayers as I stood in the pulpit the next Sunday. It is so encouraging to know an organization like yours truly cares for people like me." —ANONYMOUS CONSTITUENT

HERE TO HELP

QUIETLY REACHING OUT IN LOVE

Most people's impression of Focus comes from the broadcast, magazines, or other media resources. But there's so much more ministry and service that goes on quietly, behind the scenes.

For instance, our staff includes several chaplains whose express purpose is to reach out in love to those who are experiencing personal difficulties. Chaplains often assist through calls—praying on the phone with those who are troubled—and through resources that can minister in particular situations.

The first Focus chaplain was Warnie Tippett. When an Air Mexico plane crashed into the Pacific Ocean, Warnie did some research and called Focus constituents who had lost family members in the crash, asking how we could be of service.

This same desire to share God's love has resulted in trips to various cities whenever needs there have arisen. Coordinating efforts through pastors and churches, special teams have reached out to families and communities impacted by hurricanes, floods, school shootings, and other tragedies. The message these chaplains bring: God still cares and will provide.

Counselors and chaplains spend time on the phone encouraging and praying with the many people who contact the ministry with serious family needs.

As Dr. Dobson has explained many times on the air and in print, he is not a pastor or a theologian. He is a psychologist by choice and by training, holding a doctorate in child development from the University of Southern California. During the early years of his career and the early days of this ministry he had a private counseling practice. As Focus on the Family expanded, it was natural that we would also develop a strong component of biblically based counseling.

Many of the Focus on the Family broadcasts, films, videos, tapes, books, and magazines have offered solid, practical assistance to confused and troubled families. Dr. Dobson has often said that simply by producing such resources we have, in effect, hung out a shingle that says, "We care about you." And people have responded to that attitude by calling us when they run into difficult times.

When they call or write, their questions are referred to our Correspondence department, where each request is handled sensitively and compassionately. But in those situations involving complexities beyond the Correspondence staff's expertise, our Counseling department is asked to intervene.

This team of professionally trained, state-licensed counselors provides help in urgent situations, such as those involving potential suicides, spouse abuse, and child molestation. These pleas for help are answered one-on-one, within the context of a personal telephone call. Currently eighteen therapists spend most of each day, five days a week, on the phone with individuals who have written or called us with urgent family requests. They provide practical assistance, offer encouragement, administer the healing power of Christ's love, and pray with the folks on the other end of the line. At last count they were handling between seven hundred and nine hundred calls per week.

Often the time on the phone is all that's required to help a caller through the immediate crisis. But when additional or ongoing assistance is needed, we refer individuals to counselors and therapists around the country whose beliefs and standards are consistent with our own. These professionals have agreed to partner with us in providing consistent, face-to-face service when the concerns go beyond what we can handle by phone.

We deeply appreciate the vital role and impact a counselor can have in someone's life. In the late 1980s we began offering the Counseling Enrichment Program, an accredited program in extended education for counselors and students. Well-known Christian professionals teach and lead discussions at this highly effective seminar. General sessions and workshops emphasize the integration of psychological and biblical concepts and their application to critical issues facing today's Christian counselor. ∎

"One day I talked on the phone to a hurting constituent who said she had no hope. She kept telling me that she didn't feel God working in her life. It was an open door for me to share with her about God's love and mercy, so I asked if she wanted to receive Christ as her Lord and Savior. She said yes! We prayed together, and then I transferred her to a counselor. What a thrilling moment for me to be used by God. Focus is making a difference—and those of us in Counseling see it happen every day." —JANE STONE, COUNSELING DEPARTMENT

Sharing God's Love

Focus's counseling staff offers guidance, direction, and encouragement to people struggling with all kinds of problems. Most often the counselors work with adults who contact the ministry, but sometimes they have the opportunity to share God's love with young people.

Several years ago, a thirteen-year-old girl wrote to Focus in desperation after a failed suicide attempt. In response to her letter, a counselor called to check on her and offer help. This counselor phoned the girl every week for a month to make sure that she was doing well.

God used that counselor at a critical time in the girl's life, and years later she wrote with an update: "I am so thankful for Focus and for the counselor's efforts twelve years ago. I have a wonderful husband and a beautiful six-week-old baby. Thank you so much for your ministry—it really does help change lives."

In many situations, our counselors emphasize the principle of "tough love," which forms the basis for Dr. Dobson's book *Love Must Be Tough*. The concept urges people to stand firm for the truth, even in the midst of troubled relationships. One woman wrote to express appreciation for Dr. Dobson's book and the encouragement she received from a Focus counselor:

> Eleven years ago, I wrote you a letter out of despair and hopelessness. My marriage was falling apart due to my husband's adultery. When I received *Love Must Be Tough*, I inhaled it. One of your counselors called me and talked for over an hour and a half, praying with me and telling me, "Get ready, the change is coming. Our staff at Focus will pray for your husband and marriage, so get ready for a miracle." A few months later, my husband broke down, came to me, and confessed he'd been playing games with God. He wanted what I had—peace. We prayed together as he asked Jesus to be his Lord and Savior. ∎

Counselors meet together and pray for people who contact the ministry for help.

"In November of 1994 our one and only daughter, just nine years old, passed away. Shortly after that, I called Focus on the Family, very, very heartbroken and numb, to say the least. Praise the Lord! This gentle, kindhearted counselor listened to my terrible story. I could tell he had tears in his eyes as he spoke to me and prayed with me—he truly was sent by God to be there at that moment for me! Within the next day or two, I received a phone call from this 'earthly angel' from Focus, to talk with me once again. Even though it was my darkest hour, I will never, ever forget what this ministry did for me. Thank you!" —Amalia Colon, constituent

PART FOUR

LIGHT IN DARKNESS

Infusing Our Culture with God's Truth

A number of visitors to our headquarters have commented that seeing our buildings perched on a high knoll brought to mind the verse in Matthew 5: "You are the light of the world. A city on a hill cannot be hidden" (v. 14). It's a wonderful compliment, because that's exactly what we strive to be—a light.

Of course, the light motif is used throughout Scripture as a metaphor for how God's children should live. The passage in Matthew 5 goes on to say, "Let your light shine before men, that they may see your good deeds and praise your Father in heaven" (v. 16). At Focus, we believe Christians have both the opportunity and responsibility to bring the light of God's truth and love to our increasingly darkened culture.

Frankly, sometimes God calls us to shine a light in places we would rather not go. When Dr. Dobson began Focus twenty-five years ago, he didn't anticipate jumping into the "troubled waters of public policy." He was enjoying helping moms and dads learn to communicate, successfully raise strong-willed children, and make their homes happy and harmonious.

But as the culture wars intensified, he realized he could not stand idly by as the government, academic institutions, secular media, and other social forces eroded traditional family values and flouted God's principles. He began to speak out on important moral and public policy issues, and he soon mobilized Focus's resources to defend the family from an onslaught of attacks.

Today, the ministry uses radio, television, print and electronic media, and special events to communicate truth even when others appear unwilling to do so. We've worked hard to give people a solid foundation of biblical truth—and in doing so, Focus has become a respected source of biblical information on important issues such as the sanctity of life, the preservation of marriage, parental rights, and many others.

As we've joined with other organizations and individuals to defend the family and Christian principles in many arenas, God has faithfully used our efforts. Always, He has given us courage and strength as we have sought to represent the One who said, "I am the light of the world" (John 8:12).

Dr. Dobson was honored to be among those chosen to carry the Olympic torch as it passed through Colorado Springs on January 31, 2002, on its way to Salt Lake City.

CHANGING PUBLIC POLICY

IN 1988, A HANDFUL OF MEN sat in a Washington, D.C., hotel conference room, facing a dilemma.

The problem? Government was becoming more unfriendly to the family, and the latest evidence was on the table that day: Congress was passing bad tax and child-care policies that meant more women would be forced to leave their children to enter the workplace. And the U.S. Senate was bullying a politically incorrect Christian school, Grove City College in Pennsylvania.

Troubled by the issues, the men asked, Should Dr. Dobson stand up to this bully and risk getting his organization bruised or crippled in the culture at large? Or should he keep Focus safely tucked into the Christian subculture and enjoy its growing reputation as the premier conservative advocate for the family?

Tom Minnery, vice president of Public Policy, recalls: "I was new to Focus then, and I was in that meeting, along with other Focus staff including Senior Vice President Peb Jackson, who had been opening doors in Washington for Focus. Other participants were a businessman, and several trusted Washington Christians, all men of strong reputations. Dr. Dobson assembled the group because he wanted advice and a decision."

Some in the group were apprehensive. Could Focus press its case on national moral controversies without getting chewed up by the media? Focus had already tested the cultural waters the year before by launching *Citizen*, a monthly issues-based magazine. Lobbying government, however, was a much bigger risk.

Dr. Dobson was willing to leverage his—and Focus's—good reputation to advance Christ's cause in the public square. He just didn't want to use the influence unwisely. His film *Where's Dad?* was melting many hardened hearts in Congress, and he and the men wondered whether an aggressive lobbying effort spearheaded by Dobson would undermine the tender message of that film. But perhaps, they hoped, congressmen could be influenced on behalf of the family and ministered to at the same time. As the meeting wore on, it became obvious to all that God was guiding Dr. Dobson into a well-laid plan for addressing federal and state policies.

At top, Jerry Regier, who founded the Family Research Council, with Dr. Dobson.

Gary Bauer, middle, succeeded Jerry Regier and led FRC from 1988 to 2000.

Above, Ken Connor, the current president of FRC.

Opposite: Peb Jackson and Dr. Dobson pose outside the Capitol in Washington, D.C., after a meeting with several pro-family congressmen in the mid-1980s.

"No one has had a greater influence on conservative public policy than Dr. James Dobson. He encouraged me in the early days of the Family Research Council, and was instrumental in helping to start the organization. What influenced me the most, however, was the time we spent praying about how to proceed, asking the Lord what He wanted us to do—how He wanted us to impact the family."

—JERRY REGIER, FOUNDER OF THE FAMILY RESEARCH COUNCIL

Thus was born the Public Policy arm of Focus on the Family, and in the days since, it has branched out in many directions. The Family Research Council was fortified and expanded under new leadership by Gary Bauer, one of the participants in that first meeting, and it became Focus's voice in Washington. Tom Minnery was asked to lead the charge at Focus.

Under his leadership, our Public Policy division began several other forms of outreach including state-level family policy organizations (which now operate in nearly forty states) and a news radio feature, *Family News in Focus*.

In recent years, Focus's public policy efforts have grown tremendously. We've developed a lobbying presence at the United Nations; the "Love Won Out" ministry to help homosexuals break free from the gay lifestyle; CitizenLink, our national daily e-mail update; a consortium of activist physicians; a strategy for advancing abstinence in public schools; and a team to handle grassroots activism and mailings. We also joined several national ministries to start the Alliance Defense Fund, which defends religious freedom in the nation's courts.

"On any particular day, we might be discouraged or excited by our progress in public policy issues," Minnery says. "But we always remind ourselves that the ultimate outcome belongs to God. Most importantly, we are thankful to Him for His clear leading in this area of our ministry. His guidance has allowed the name of Focus on the Family to remain high in stature and not be diminished by our role in confronting the unwise policies of government." ∎

Dr. Dobson was a frequent guest in the Oval Office during both the Reagan and George H. W. Bush administrations. At top, in a one-on-one meeting with the elder George Bush in May 1988.

Both Dr. and Shirley Dobson have also met with President George W. Bush, above, to encourage his stand on pro-family and pro-life issues.

Bob Ditmer and Jimmy Peck in the Public Policy studio, left, preparing to record *Family News in Focus*.

Dr. Dobson, opposite, with President Reagan.

ISSUES OF INFLUENCE

In November 1987, Focus on the Family launched *Citizen*, a monthly magazine that motivates readers to become involved in city, state, and federal issues affecting the family, often encouraging them to contact their senators and congressmen when these legislators are considering significant bills.

Tom Minnery, vice president of Public Policy, recalls how the publication came into being:

I met with Dr. Dobson in 1987 to discuss a book I had edited on the harms of pornography. I expressed my surprise at the number of churches that wanted me to speak on the subject. Pornography—what a topic for church! Dr. Dobson told me he wished Focus had a way to communicate more often about such issues. He asked if I would put together a mock-up of a magazine addressing public policy issues. I did, and the Focus leadership team loved it, the board approved it, and I joined Focus to start it.

I named it *Citizen* to denote the fact that in our country Christians have as much say in governmental affairs as anyone, and citizenship is a duty to be fulfilled. The magazine's focus is on grassroots America as much as on Washington, because in local communities active Christian people are winning moral battles all the time.

With this in mind, articles frequently go beyond legislative issues. *Citizen* regularly presents stories on education, the media, and the arts, as well as profiles and interviews with both well-known newsmakers and lesser-known activists—"hometown heroes," as we call them.

Over the years, we've been continually gratified by the way in which our readers have been moved to action. In fact, *Citizen* has become such an influential, integral part of our ministry that in October 1993, the magazine branched out to include Citizen Issues Alert, a weekly fax publication that provides timely updates not afforded by a monthly magazine. Then, in March 1998, Focus launched its web counterpart, CitizenLink, which has become one of the most visited portals on the Focus website, providing up-to-the-minute details on public policy issues, including contact information for legislators on key questions related to the family. ∎

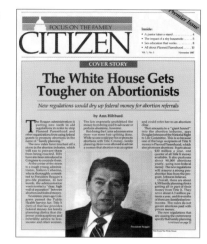

Above, the first issue of *Citizen* magazine, 1987. The magazine has changed its look and added color since its inception, but its mission has remained constant.

Tom Hess, left, the current editor of *Citizen*.

Opposite: Tom Minnery, vice president of Public Policy, addresses a gathering at the Focus headquarters in Colorado Springs.

FAMILY POLICY COUNCILS

NATIONAL LEGISLATION AND POLICY DEBATES may garner the most media attention, but issues at state and local levels can have an enormous impact on families as well. Consequently, over the past fourteen years we have supported statewide organizations whose Christian principles reflect our own. These Family Policy Councils are distinct from Focus, coordinated by separate boards of directors. But they draw on our research and resources to positively impact their communities and states.

Family Policy Councils have grown tremendously since their inception in 1988, currently existing in nearly forty states. For years, many of the councils sent a newsletter to their members along with an issue of *Citizen* magazine until e-mail and web sites became more convenient communications tools. These organizations have successfully introduced family-friendly legislation and counteracted bills detrimental to traditional values.

John Paulton, the former executive director of the South Dakota Family Policy Council, explains how Focus often assists these state organizations: "In 1995, Hawaii was on the verge of legalizing same-sex marriage, and Focus helped defeat it. In response, we in South Dakota had tried and failed to pass legislation to ensure that recognized marriage remained only between a man and a woman. As we geared up for a new effort in 1996, Focus realized that our effort had huge national implications."

Focus developed a campaign to alert South Dakotans to the critical nature of the legislation, sending thousands of letters to South Dakota homes. We also devoted radio broadcasts, fax alerts, and church bulletin inserts to the issue.

"As a result, the people of South Dakota spoke to their legislators in unprecedented numbers, urging them to pass this marriage-protection legislation," says Paulton, who is now a staff member in the Family Policy Council area of Focus's Public Policy division. "After defeating the bill the previous year, the state legislature passed the bill in 1996 by an overwhelming margin. But that was just the beginning: Since then, thirty states have passed similar legislation protecting marriage."

Above, just a few of the state inserts created by Family Policy Councils and included in *Citizen* magazine.

At right, a group of Family Policy Council directors at Focus for the 2001 Directors' Conference.

Opposite: Rocky Mountain Family Council Executive Director Jim Chapman and Legislative Liaison Sharon Johnson pose at the Colorado state capitol after testifying on Internet safety legislation.

God's work has truly been evident in these Family Policy Councils. Gary Palmer of the Alabama Policy Institute remembers the dramatic—and unexpected—way the Lord led him to start up the Alabama organization: "My journey into the arena of public policy began with a *Focus on the Family* broadcast in March 1989, in which Dr. Dobson told his listeners about the Counseling Enrichment Program, held that summer at Focus."

The program was open to licensed counselors, ministers, and graduate students pursuing a counseling degree—and had only twenty-five participants at that. Gary didn't meet any of the criteria and knew that if he applied, he'd have to resign from his job as an engineer. "Yet my wife, Ann, insisted that I apply," he said. "She reminded me I'd been praying for God to direct my path and open doors for me. So acting on the faith of my wife, I did."

Gary was admitted to the program, and soon after found himself in Pomona, California, still unsure why he was there. "After three weeks of classes on topics I knew nothing about, I thought, 'Palmer, you've lost your mind. You quit your job for a counseling conference.'"

But during the fourth week he met with Randy Hicks, the central region public policy representative for Focus, who was looking to establish some contacts in Alabama. Gary suggested that Focus develop state or regional extensions of the ministry. Randy was floored. That was exactly what Focus was already trying to do—help establish independent state-based family policy organizations all over the nation. "At that point," Gary recalls, "I knew why God had sent me to Focus."

With no experience in the public policy arena, Gary agreed to help start a Family Policy Council in Alabama: the Alabama Family Alliance—now the Alabama Policy Institute. In 1990, he became executive director.

"In less than two years, God had raised up a man of no reputation to lead what has since become one of the most successful state-based policy organizations in the country," he marvels. "The Alabama Policy Institute has worked on everything from abstinence and environmental education to even the amazing defeat of the lottery. It all began with a radio broadcast I thought was for a counseling program—but God used it as a divine appointment." ∎

The staffs of Focus and the Capitol Resource Institute pose at top with volunteers in Los Angeles following a successful rally protesting teacher union policies.

Above, Alabama Policy Institute Director Gary Palmer and his family.

Opposite: Some participants at a Los Angeles rally organized by California's Capitol Resource Institute and Focus's Public Policy staff.

"Focus and Dr. Dobson have been the light on the hill, always standing for God's truth and fighting for the cause of righteousness. Thank you, Focus, and thank you, Jim and Shirley, for all that you have done for millions of families and for the advancement of the Lord's Kingdom. We love you." —BOB HAMBY [CPA AND FOCUS ON THE FAMILY BOARD MEMBER] AND REBECCA HAMBY

TAKING A STAND

Sheri and Jerry Anderson with their children (left to right), Samantha, Alana, and Rebecca.

Opposite: Focus on the Family often provides phone numbers and mailing and e-mail addresses to help people let their elected officials know where they stand on important issues.

WITH SO MANY MOMENTOUS public policy issues affecting families, it's sometimes tempting for Christians to concentrate only on our immediate struggles and lose sight of the big picture—influencing the world for Christ. But then we'll receive a letter such as this, which helps keep things in perspective:

Dear Tom Minnery,

Today, I finally began working through my huge stack of paperwork. Surveys, insurance forms, bills, and the like have a way of piling up when you have three children under age five!

When I came to your letter about the three issues currently before the Pennsylvania General Assembly, I sighed. "Another time-consuming thing I need to do," I thought. Being a Christian, however, I knew I couldn't just throw it away and move on. After all, these are the things that will make a difference a hundred years from now.

So I got the phone book, not having a clue who my state legislators are. Meanwhile, the children wanted a snack, my husband needed me to help retrieve the dog and bring her inside, and the table was covered with papers. . . . But I told myself that calling was the right thing to do. I called my representative, then my senator, then Governor Ridge's office. I told the receptionist at the governor's office I had a letter from Focus on the Family and I wanted to give my opinion on three issues.

She said, "I bet I know which ones." Then she proceeded to tell me what the issues were, which I confirmed. She informed me she didn't know why, but she had a thirty-page list of people from all across the state who had called to tell her the same thing.

I told her about your letter, which described the bills and what action we should take. She thought it was wonderful that an organization would do this. More importantly, she said that every one of the people on all thirty pages was just like me—very friendly and polite. No one screamed or yelled at her. I explained that we are Christians and we represent Jesus, and I was glad to hear we were doing it so well. She was impressed!

I thought it would encourage you to know that many people are responding to your plea to stand up and be counted. They are making a difference for Jesus. I also wanted to thank you for taking time to compile a letter that makes it simple for those of us who are overworked and frazzled.

Sheri Anderson
Middletown, Pennsylvania

"Before listening to Focus on the Family, I was not much interested in political issues. Now I make sure I vote in every election, and I pay attention to family issues. I have been able to call attention to family issues to friends and family who were otherwise unaware." —NIKKOL HARPER, CONSTITUENT

SIGNS OF ENCOURAGEMENT

Billboards advertise a priceless commodity

□ Campaign's goal is to get drivers to think about family values

By MICHAEL MILLER
of the Journal Star

PEORIA — Have you had an unusual urge while driving the streets and highways of the Tri-County Area lately to hug your kids or to treat the family to a night out?

Or have you just been wondering what the deal is with all those "family" billboards?

The billboard campaign is both a public service effort by Adams Outdoor Advertising and an effort by Focus on the Family to get people focusing on . . . well, the family.

The national Christian ministry, based in Colorado Springs, Colo., sent requests for ad space to outdoor advertising companies nationwide, and Adams responded with $15,000 worth of space, said Bob Lord, Adams' general manager.

Adams has put up about 30 of the billboard posters — which were printed by Focus on the Family — since January. They will stay up positively through mid-March, Lord said, as paid space is needed. None may stay up longer.

Nationally, about $4 million of ad space has been donated, according to Focus on the Family.

"It's kind of a no-brainer," Lord said. "Obviously it's a very important issue and something our community feels strongly about. These are the kind of things you want up, and we certainly support this kind of message."

Adams typically devotes between 3 and 5 percent of its inventory — 15 to 20 billboards — a month to public service announcements, Lord said.

"There carry so many causes that are worthwhile," he said.

Lord said the posters were simply put up where space was available. Some of them ended up in fairly high-traffic areas, such as Farmington Road near Bradley Park and on main thoroughfares near downtown.

The goal, said Focus director of corporate marketing John Thompson, "is to get people to think about family."

There are two posters on display, one showing a father tightening a tie on his son with the words "Family . . . Ties That Bind!" superimposed. The other shows a family of four's beaming faces between the words "Family . . . High Yield Bonds."

"The family is the basic unit of life in the United States," Thompson said. "Everybody wants to be connected, everybody wants to feel a part of something, and the family is the building block that God has provided to help fill that need.

"Dialing out any kind of religious connotation, what's the family really all about? That's what it is."

The campaign is in its second year after Charlie Renfroe, an Atlanta outdoor advertising executive, asked Focus if it would like to put its pro-family message on billboards across the country last year.

"We just simply followed up on that and were able to expand it this year," Thompson said, adding that Renfroe's contacts in the industry "were key."

While the message is to strengthen family bonds, Focus on the Family's name and toll-free phone number is also on the posters.

"Really, that's the response desire for people if they have questions about who we are," Thompson said, or if they need help with a family situation or crisis. With 260 people stationed by phones "all the time," Thompson said, "a number of the calls that we receive deal with crisis intervention."

"We can route these calls to our master-level counselors that we have on staff.

"By far the majority of them are asking for resources. We have lots of free information."

It doesn't hurt in getting some free advertising for Focus, though, right?

"You know, that's true," Thompson said, "but as a nonprofit ministry, what we are interested in primarily is if we do get our name out there," people will be aware of "a free resource."

People also sent photos of billboards last year to give Focus an idea of the context of the posters' display, Thompson said.

"In a couple of areas, a billboard was posted adjacent to an adult night club," he said. "That tells me that God has a sense of humor.

"More than anything else, it's a message for people headed into that business. Maybe it stopped a couple of people from having to go in there.

"Ultimately, if this kind of thing is even beneficial from a standpoint of making people think, 'My family is important, my time at work is not more vital than with my family, I need to spend time at home with my family,' it would be all worthwhile."

Above, one of many articles that appeared in cities nationwide as Focus issued press releases to draw attention to family messages.

Right and opposite: Some of the billboards that appeared in major cities during the campaign.

Over the years, we've been encouraged by the many ways in which God has enabled us to communicate His message for families. One great friend of the ministry, Charlie Renfroe, came up with a brilliant method to reach people who may not otherwise know about Focus on the Family.

"It all started one evening in June 1996, when we were talking at Elk Canyon [a Focus retreat in the mountains]," explains Charlie. "One of the men had just shown us some samples of the new *Focus on the Family Commentary* produced for TV, and we thought they were terrific. At that time, I was the owner of a major advertising agency in Atlanta, and I told Dr. Dobson, 'If you can get that message into ten words or less, I can put it on a billboard!'"

Dr. Dobson loved the idea, and Peak Creative, Focus's in-house creative group, designed the signs. Charlie promoted the concept to other billboard owners on behalf of the ministry, asking them to post the messages when their boards were between advertisers. That went over so well, he asked other friends in the advertising industry to join him in spreading God's truth about the importance of family. So many were eager to promote a positive message and do something for public service that some even paid to put up the boards!

"All together, we placed four to five thousand boards nationwide in 1997 and even more in 1998," recalls Charlie. "A lot of people asked for larger bulletins, the big billboards you see by freeways—and some of those stayed up for six months!" All of the billboards that were

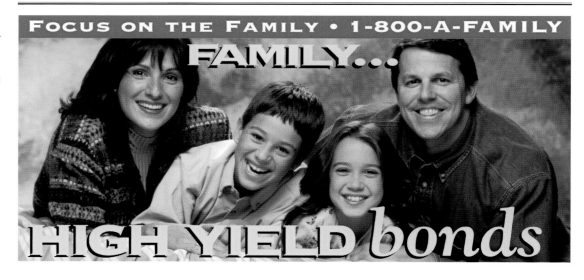

FOCUS ON THE FAMILY • 1-800-A-FAMILY
FAMILY...
HIGH YIELD bonds

donated across the country would have cost us more than $2.5 million if we'd had to purchase that space. We received hundreds of calls from people who had seen the signs, and a number of people were made aware of Focus for the first time.

There were other benefits. Many billboard operators were invited to speak to local groups because of the family ads, giving them a chance to share Focus's message. And the ministry put out press releases in many cities, which resulted in a wave of media exposure.

"We hope and pray that many people began a relationship with Jesus Christ as a result of hearing about the ministry of Focus on the Family," says Charlie. "God did so much more than we ever thought possible. It's exciting to see what can happen when you listen to Him and obey His call!" ∎

Charlie Renfroe, who proposed the billboard idea to Dr. Dobson, with his wife and eight grandchildren.

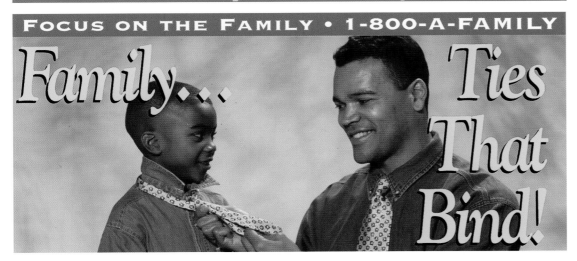

"If my people, who are called by my name, will humble themselves and pray and seek my face and turn from their wicked ways, then will I hear from heaven and will forgive their sin and will heal their land." 2 CHRONICLES 7:14

NATIONAL DAY OF PRAYER

PRAYER IS AN INTEGRAL PART of America's spiritual heritage. For more than fifty years, our calendar has included a National Day of Prayer. This observance, held on the first Thursday of every May, is currently overseen from Focus on the Family's headquarters.

Although the National Day of Prayer (NDP) Task Force is a separate and distinct nonprofit organization responsible for its own fund-raising, Focus and NDP are sister ministries that share the same facilities. The Focus board of directors has embraced the National Day of Prayer Task Force and contributed to its early development. Since 1991, Shirley Dobson has served as chairperson of the NDP Task Force.

"There is nothing more dear to my heart than prayer," she says.

The NDP Task Force hosts the event in Washington, D.C. Representatives of the military and all three branches of the government participate in an observance filled with prayer and patriotism.

"However, when Vonette Bright, the former chairperson of the National Day of Prayer, first asked me to assume her position, I was hesitant. I explained to her that my responsibilities at Focus on the Family prevented me from being able to tackle an assignment of this magnitude. Looking back now, I realize that I didn't just close the door on the possibility. . . . I slammed it shut!"

In the weeks that followed, Mrs. Dobson heard God saying, "Shirley, you didn't ask Me about your decision." Convicted, she began praying that God would clearly reveal His will to her by confirming it both through her husband and through Mrs. Bright.

She first asked her husband for his opinion. "I was sure he would say that such a commitment wasn't a good idea in light of our numerous other obligations," she recalls. "But when I approached him, Jim said, 'Shirley, what more important ministry is there than calling the nation to prayer?' I was amazed by his response! However, I continued to pray, still not certain of God's plan."

People of all ages, races, and denominations join together in local prayer events.

Opposite: The events of September 11, 2001, have united young and old together in prayer for our communities, our country, and our world, leading people to seek the God of peace.

Colorado Springs's local newspaper, *The Gazette*, featured a story on Shirley Dobson and the National Day of Prayer in April 1995. Shirley is pictured with family dog Mitzy.

Above, Mrs. Dobson addresses the audience inside the Cannon House Office Building during the annual National Day of Prayer observance in Washington, D.C.

Opposite: Shirley Dobson presents a bound copy of all fifty state proclamations to President George W. Bush during the May 2001 National Day of Prayer.

Specifically, Shirley prayed that if this ministry opportunity was right for her, Mrs. Bright would ask her to reconsider—even after having been flatly turned down. Several weeks passed, and the Dobsons met with Vonette and her husband, Dr. Bill Bright (founder of Campus Crusade for Christ), for dinner.

"To my surprise," Mrs. Dobson recalls, "Vonette reiterated her thoughts, saying, 'Bill and I have continued to pray and still feel that you are God's choice for the National Day of Prayer.' With this further evidence of the Lord's direction, I told Vonette that I would get back to her within one week. During my quiet times over the next few days, God affirmed that He wanted me to accept the assignment."

When Shirley assumed her new position, the NDP Task Force had one volunteer and a meager budget of $6,000. Today, more than forty thousand volunteers organize thirty thousand prayer observances in every state in the union, and NDP has a budget of $1.5 million. Millions of Americans participated in NDP events in 2001—the fiftieth anniversary of the occasion.

While a national observance takes place in Washington, D.C., each year, the lifeblood of NDP flows through communities nationwide as Americans humbly pray for our country and its leaders. Volunteers have transformed NDP into a powerful grassroots movement, organizing prayer gatherings in churches, parks, schools, and other public venues from coast to coast.

The explosive growth of NDP—under Mrs. Dobson's leadership—is a powerful reminder of God's faithfulness. She concludes, "While the task remains daunting at times, the lesson I've learned is that the will of God will never take you where His grace cannot keep you. As 2 Corinthians 12:9 reminds us, His power is made perfect in our weakness." ∎

"Our teachers have an annual prayer breakfast on the National Day of Prayer, with two to three hundred in attendance every year. It is a blessing to see public school teachers and administrators circle together with their heads bowed, asking for God's direction in the schools. I'm thrilled to have been the founding chairperson of this prayer breakfast, and I hope we can spread this involvement to other school districts across the nation." —FREDDA ROSENBAUM, CONSTITUENT

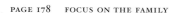

A Chance to Speak Out for Family Issues

Over the years, Dr. Dobson has had the privilege of serving on several federal commissions and committees:

Appointed delegate-at-large to the Los Angeles White House Conference on Families, June 1980.

Appointed to the Task Force for the White House Conferences on Families, August 1980. Authored a minority report that became part of the final document.

Received a special commendation from President Jimmy Carter for work on the White House Conferences on Families, September 1980.

Appointed by President Ronald Reagan to the National Advisory Commission for the Office of Juvenile Justice and Delinquency Prevention, 1982–1986.

Appointed by Attorney General Edwin Meese to the Commission on Pornography, May 1985–October 1986.

Co-chaired the Citizens Advisory Panel for Tax Reform, 1985–1986, in consultation with President Ronald Reagan.

Served as a member of the United States Army Task Force on Families, appointed by Chief of Staff General John Wickham, 1986–1987, and as chairman in 1988.

Appointed by Attorney General Edwin Meese to the Attorney General's Advisory Board on Missing and Exploited Children, 1987–1988.

Appointed by Secretary Otis Bowen to the Department of Health and Human Services Panel on Teen Pregnancy Prevention, 1987–1988.

Appointed by Senator Robert Dole to the Commission on Child and Family Welfare, 1994–1996.

Appointed by Senate Majority Leader Trent Lott to the National Gambling Impact and Study Commission, 1996–1998.

A Call to Prayer

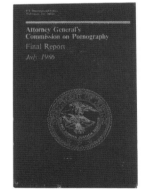

God has responded to our prayers during times of crisis. One such time occurred in the mid-1980s, when Dr. Dobson was serving on the Attorney General's Commission on Pornography. The appointed members tilted in a liberal direction, and it seemed likely from the beginning that the final report would fail to expose the awful reality of pornography, with its overwhelming tendency to destroy families.

After eighteen months of arduous deliberation and hearings, the commission created two reports: one a forty-page whitewash of pornography, and the other a two-thousand-page document showing the full depravity of this curse and suggesting signpost changes in the law.

"I had sat through enough testimony to understand just how dark and satanic this multibillion-dollar industry really is," Dr. Dobson says. "And I was convinced that pornography really is progressive and addictive in nature—that it destroys families and fosters unthinkable forms of child abuse. It was a bad situation. The few conservative members of the group were up against a stacked deck."

Two days before the commission ended, Dr. Dobson appeared to be the lone voice in support of the longer report. When a straw vote was taken, the result was ten to one in favor of the whitewashed version. Recognizing the seriousness of the spiritual battle, he called to ask the Focus staff to unite in fasting and prayer.

That afternoon, three hundred Focus employees fasted and prayed on behalf of Dr. Dobson and the commission. When the members reconvened the next morning for their final vote, the most influential commissioner rose to speak. He said he'd had difficulty sleeping the night before as he wrestled with the meaning of pornography.

"For the first time, this psychiatrist, who made no profession of faith, said he realized that obscenity is a moral issue and that our final report should reflect not just the proper interpretation of the First Amendment, but also the issue of rightness and wrongness," Dr. Dobson recalls. "He spoke eloquently on behalf of the longer, more complete report that dealt with the evil of the pornographic industry."

When the commissioner had finished speaking, another vote was taken, and the two-thousand-page report was accepted unanimously. Twenty-six recommendations for changes in the law were put forward, and in the months that followed, every one of them was passed by Congress and signed into law by President Reagan. Some of the most notorious porn kings, such as billionaire Reuben Sturman, were charged, tried, and convicted of obscenity. Some of them remain in prison to this day.

Dr. Dobson sums up the dramatic turn of events: "Can it be scientifically proven that this remarkable overnight reversal of the commissioners' attitudes was the direct result of prayer? Of course not. But for those who have eyes to see, there's no other explanation to account for the facts. Prayer really does change things. Here at Focus on the Family, we know that it's true!" ■

At top, members of the former attorney general Edwin Meese's Commission on Pornography, 1985.

The commission's report, above, was issued after eighteen months of work.

Opposite: Focus staff and volunteers brave cold temperatures on November 3, 2000, as they surround the buildings in a circle of prayer, following a time of prayer and repentance indoors after several weeks of discouraging news in the organization.

FOCUS ON THE MILITARY FAMILY

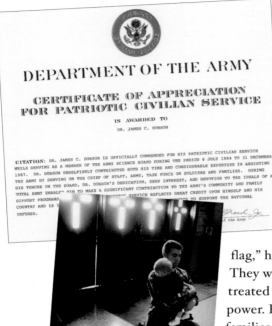

DEPARTMENT OF THE ARMY

CERTIFICATE OF APPRECIATION
FOR PATRIOTIC CIVILIAN SERVICE

IS AWARDED TO

DR. JAMES C. DOBSON

CITATION: DR. JAMES C. DOBSON IS OFFICIALLY COMMENDED FOR HIS PATRIOTIC CIVILIAN SERVICE
WHILE SERVING AS A MEMBER OF THE ARMY SCIENCE BOARD DURING THE PERIOD 8 JULY 1984 TO 31 DECEMBER
1987. DR. DOBSON UNSELFISHLY CONTRIBUTED BOTH HIS TIME AND CONSIDERABLE EXPERTISE IN ASSISTING
THE ARMY BY SERVING ON THE CHIEF OF STAFF, ARMY, TASK FORCE ON SOLDIERS AND FAMILIES. DURING
HIS TENURE ON THE BOARD, DR. DOBSON'S DEDICATION, DEEP INTEREST, AND DEVOTION TO THE IDEALS OF A
TOTAL ARMY ENABLED HIM TO MAKE A SIGNIFICANT CONTRIBUTION TO THE ARMY'S COMMUNITY AND FAMILY
SUPPORT PROGRAMS. ... ... SERVICE REFLECTS GREAT CREDIT UPON HIMSELF AND HIS
COUNTRY AND IS ... ... TO SUPPORT THE NATIONAL
DEFENSE.

Above, Dr. Dobson received the Certificate of Appreciation for Patriotic Civilian Service from the Department of the Army in 1987 for his contribution to the army's community and family support program.

Opposite: General John A. Wickham, U.S. army chief of staff from 1983 to 1987, was committed to the welfare of army families during his tenure. General Wickham appointed Dr. Dobson to the U.S. Army Family Initiative from 1986 to 1988. Dr. Dobson spoke to all of the three- and four-star generals in a Pentagon briefing in 1987.

RAISING CHILDREN AND MAINTAINING A STRONG MARRIAGE isn't easy, but men and women in uniform often face even greater pressure than the average family, from going on dangerous assignments to leaving home for months on end. In 1984 Dr. Dobson was invited to the Pentagon to confer with General John Wickham, then army chief of staff, to discuss the state of military families and how to strengthen them.

Dr. Dobson, Shirley, and Ryan spent the day with General Wickham and his wife, Ann, at Quarters One, the historic house where every chief of staff has lived since 1903. The general's office in the Pentagon was adorned with almost 150 flags and banners commemorating every battle ever fought in American history.

But Dr. Dobson remembers even more vividly the kindness he showed to Ryan. "General Wickham gave him a knife and his own personal flag," he says. "He and his staff devoted an incredible amount of time to this little boy. They were important men, with stars on their shoulders and on their hats. But they treated Ryan with dignity and respect. They hold the reins of military authority and power. But they are also very compassionate men—family men. They care about army families and they're trying to do something to help them."

In response to General Wickham's appeal for help, Focus initiated a new effort to minister to military families. We wanted to let these families know that we recognize the pressures they face, we care about them, and we have materials available to address their specific needs.

Since the mid-1980s, a weekly variation of the *Focus on the Family* radio program has aired on the Armed Forces Radio & Television Services Network (AFRTS). This feature is distributed from their headquarters by satellite, compact disc, and short-wave radio to every U.S. military installation around the world and to all ships at sea. Hundreds of copies of the *Where's Dad?* special were purchased for military bases around the world, with an order from General Wickham that every member of the U.S. army would see it. Many other Focus resources have been made available through the years.

God has indeed been at work among our military families! Over the years, we've found that the following statement by General Douglas MacArthur summarizes the attitude of many of our country's military leaders:

> By profession, I'm a soldier, and I take great pride in that fact. But I am prouder, infinitely prouder, to be a father. A soldier destroys in order to build. A father only builds, never destroys. ...It is my hope that my son, when I'm gone, will remember me, not from the battle, but in the home, repeating with him our simple daily prayer, "Our Father, Who art in heaven."

We consider it a privilege to offer assistance to men and women in uniform as they care for their own families while serving our great country. ∎

To Dr. Jim Dobora
with deep appreciation for your US our
inspiring and valuable support
TO Army family programs
John Wickham
Chief of Staff
US Army 1987

"One day I was at a National Religious Broadcasters meeting where Dr. Dobson was speaking. With tears in his eyes, he spoke passionately for the unborn and for moral righteousness. What he said was so bold, so convicting, and really so unpopular with the political correctness of today's world that I was taken aback. His great resolve strengthened me, and his thoughts resonated with what I felt God was telling me."

—Dr. Adrian Rogers, senior pastor of Bellvue Baptist Church in Memphis, Tennessee, and Focus on the Family board member

LIFE IS SACRED

THROUGHOUT OUR TWENTY-FIVE-YEAR HISTORY, God has continually guided us into new avenues of ministry, often through the wise counsel of our board of directors. But only on rare occasions has the Lord clearly and urgently directed Dr. Dobson—and ultimately, Focus—to take specific action on an issue.

"One instance dates back to the beginning of the ministry, when the plight of preborn children was heavy on my heart," Dr. Dobson recalls. "That was early in the pro-life movement when few evangelical leaders or churches were talking about the tragedy of abortion. The Catholic church stood almost alone in its defense of the innocent during that era. But the Lord was clearly talking to me about it. Whenever I would try to explain my concern for babies, I felt a wave of sorrow. There were times when I found it difficult to continue speaking. This is why I have done everything I could in the intervening years to give a voice to the voiceless. I will do that until my days are over, or until preborn babies are again safe in their mothers' wombs."

It's not surprising, then, that the sanctity of human life is one of the five "pillars"—or fundamental principles—upon which Focus on the Family was established. Scripture teaches that each person is of inestimable worth, and Psalm 139:13 tells us that even the tiniest of preborn infants are precious in God's sight. The value of life is a conviction we passionately uphold in the public square, and it is a belief that prompted us to launch our ministry to Crisis Pregnancy Centers (CPCs).

Focus seeks to support CPCs by providing information, booklets, advice, conferences, seminars and, most importantly, prayer. Our goal is to strengthen and support those people dedicated to assisting mothers and saving preborn babies. A cornerstone of this outreach is our annual conference for CPC directors. During this gathering, participants from all over the nation share effective strategies, empathize about the challenges, and rejoice in the successes of their work.

Sometimes our own staff has the opportunity to help those facing unexpected pregnancies. We feel privileged to assist them. All too often, young mothers-to-be do not have the opportunity to hear both sides of the issue. They feel their options are extremely limited, and fear and shame drive them toward abortion. Frequently, a desperate woman will call Focus as a last resort, and our caring, trained representatives connect her with a local CPC or physician. This simple interaction is often the first step toward restoring hope to a mother and ensuring a future for her child.

We are delighted when we hear how our ministry has helped to save a baby. For instance, Focus once received a call from a distressed father who had discovered that his eighteen-year-old daughter was pregnant. Our CPC department prayed for this man and his family and provided materials to help guide them through their difficult decisions. Several months later, the man called to give a follow-up report: His daughter had given birth to a beautiful little girl, and the baby's father and mother had decided to marry. The young couple had also made a commitment to return to church and dedicate their child to the Lord. This and many other "happy ending" stories make all of our endeavors worthwhile! ■

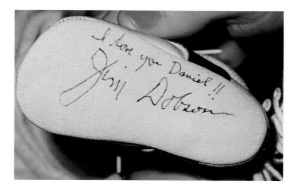

At top, a personal message from Dr. Dobson to one of the babies at a Crisis Pregnancy Center (CPC) conference. Good music, inspiring speakers, and warm fellowship are key parts of the conference agenda.

One of the younger attendees, opposite, at a recent CPC conference held at Focus's headquarters in Colorado Springs.

PHYSICIANS RESOURCE COUNCIL

GIVEN DR. DOBSON'S YEARS at the USC School of Medicine and Children's Hospital, he has long understood how physical and emotional well-being can affect families. In an effort to promote healthy families—healthy in body as well as in mind and spirit—Focus has consistently devoted radio airtime for programs dealing with medical issues.

As the response to such broadcasts grew—and the topics we addressed became more complex—it became obvious that we needed a group of medical professionals to ensure accuracy and current research data. In October 1987, a group of twenty-five physicians met with Dr. Dobson to talk about medical issues as well as how Focus might minister to doctors' families, which face unique pressures and challenges. From those discussions, the Physicians Resource Council (PRC) was formed as an advisory panel composed of specialists in a variety of disciplines. The PRC advises Dr. Dobson and Focus staff on medical issues and reviews all health-related broadcasts, films, and print resources for accuracy. The council also meets twice each year to discuss medical issues that impact the family.

These doctors have conducted a significant amount of research for us on medical and ethical issues. They have also helped put on several conferences for physicians and their spouses. The Physicians' Conferences provide times of refreshment, encouragement, and spiritual regeneration for many of the dedicated professionals whose lives are focused on the needs of others.

Over the years, the PRC has provided Focus with tangible and accessible information that families can utilize in their own homes. From 1995 to 1997, members of the PRC collaborated with the editor of our *Physician* magazine to develop the *Complete Book of Baby & Child Care*. This comprehensive volume gives parents a balanced view of their children's health issues and developmental concerns within a biblical context.

Dr. J. Thomas Fitch, a pediatrician from San Antonio, Texas, has served on the PRC since its inception. "I've been privileged to serve as an adviser to Focus, and this relationship has given me so much in return," he says. "Focus's outreach to physicians has encouraged literally thousands of medical professionals like me to view our work as a ministry—to use our influence to uphold traditional values and promote biblical principles. I will be eternally grateful to Jim Dobson and Focus for the incredible impact they have had on my spiritual, family, and professional life. I feel truly blessed to have been able to witness firsthand how God has been at work at Focus on the Family for the past twenty-five years." ■

At top, a 1996 photo of the Physicians Resource Council (PRC) and their spouses at one of the group's semiannual meetings.

Above, the PRC poses on the balcony at Focus in 1997.

Physicians Resource Council members collaborated with our editorial staff to create the *Complete Book of Baby & Child Care*, at right. More than 200,000 books have been sold to date.

Opposite: More than eight hundred medical professionals and many of their spouses attended a Physicians' Conference at Focus for a time of encouragement and challenge.

A DIVINE APPOINTMENT

Physicians often mention how much they appreciate the resources we provide to strengthen their families and spiritual lives. And our constituents regularly express their gratitude toward the doctors who volunteer their time and expertise to help Focus. But often our staff members benefit from the relationship, too. Diane Mitchell, who assists Dr. Dobson, tells how God orchestrated a divine appointment when she needed it most.

"When my dad was rediagnosed with cancer, I felt very helpless since I couldn't be there during this critical time," she says. "Shortly after the diagnosis, I received a call from a physician who wanted to register for an upcoming Physicians' Conference. When I asked what his area of expertise was, he said, 'radiology-oncology.' I chuckled and thought to myself, 'I sure would like to talk to this doctor about Dad.' Instead, I said, 'How interesting. My family is dealing with cancer issues right now.'"

The doctor immediately picked up on Diane's need for help and started asking questions: who in her family had cancer, what type, and so on.

"When I gave him a brief description of the situation, he explained about an experimental surgery that my sister had also just found out about the weekend before," she continues. "He gave me questions to ask my dad's doctor in Iowa about this type of surgery, and he suggested a new type of post-surgery body scan to tell where any new cancer spots may be popping up. This doctor's expertise and encouragement came at a critical time. God knew what I needed at that moment."

Love Won Out

Focus on the Family's "Love Won Out" ministry began in 1998 as a nation-wide outreach to educate pastors, mental-health professionals, legislators, educators, and hurting families about homosexuality. Most importantly, however, the ministry reaches men and women who find themselves trapped in the bondage of homosexuality. The goal is to convey God's truth: that His love can transform the life of any gay person. Led by Homosexuality and Gender Department Manager John Paulk and Youth and Gender Analyst Mike Haley, the team enlists the assistance of the world's foremost authorities on homosexuality.

Before joining Focus's effort, John and his wife, Anne, were national spokespersons in the ex-gay movement who had been profiled by such media as *60 Minutes*, *Oprah*, and *Newsweek*. John, who had successfully relinquished his gay lifestyle years before, had the challenge of creating the ministry's first department devoted to homosexual issues, a vital duty given the onslaught of misinformation influencing American culture.

Mike brought a similar background to the team. He began his struggle out of twelve years of homosexuality after being overcome by God's call in Jeremiah 15:19: "If you repent, I will restore you that you may serve me; if you utter worthy, not worthless, words, you will be

John Paulk and his wife, Anne, told their story of leaving the homosexual lifestyle in the book *Love Won Out* and in many national publications.

my spokesman." Mike spent the next six years ministering to others struggling to overcome homosexuality. After marrying in 1994, he worked as a youth pastor and then joined Focus in 1998.

Since the first Love Won Out conference in November 1998, homosexual activists have strongly protested the events. When a nationally known lesbian advocate and writer attended one event, John approached her as she tried to slip out the door unnoticed. "I know it took a lot of courage to even walk into this building," he told her. Her defensive posture melted away.

Two weeks later, she called. She was passing through Colorado Springs and wanted to meet with Mike and John. The details of their conversation appeared in national gay magazines and newspapers. Despite her disagreement with Focus's views, she praised the genuineness of their intentions.

Such positive dialogue is the exception, though. Given the controversial and often contentious debates over homosexuality, Paulk, Haley, and their colleagues often encounter hostility and hatred.

"Our lives and the lives of our spouses and children are often threatened," Paulk says. "The media routinely discredits our testimonies. We are misunderstood, mocked, and maligned. Yet we willingly pay the price for the privilege of seeing even one homosexual set free." ∎

Mike Haley and his wife, Angie, with their son, Bennett, at top.

Above, Mike is interviewed by local reporters after a Love Won Out event.

Opposite: The Paulks pictured with their sons, Timothy (left) and Alexander.

CONFERENCES

Women crowd outside the arena, top, before a Renewing the Heart event in Nashville, 1998. More than seventeen thousand attended.

Above, nearly fifteen thousand women filled the Alamo Dome in San Antonio, Texas, in 1998.

Below: Shirley Dobson (left) and Anne Graham Lotz (middle) spoke at several Renewing the Heart events. Many speakers drew an emotional response from conference attendees.

Opposite: Dr. Dobson was a surprise guest at several Renewing the Heart events, and offered words of welcome and encouragement to all who were there.

EACH YEAR, FOCUS ON THE FAMILY HOSTS several conferences at our headquarters, in the Chapelteria and adjacent meeting rooms. These large-scale meetings usually accommodate up to eight hundred attendees. Our conferences have featured such well-known speakers as Charles Colson, Bruce Wilkinson, John Trent, and Kay Coles James, and are designed to provide encouragement and instruction. Gatherings have been held for legislators, physicians, attorneys, mature adults, Crisis Pregnancy Center staff members, National Day of Prayer coordinators, Family Policy Council leaders, educators, and other groups.

We consider conference attendees to be our guests, and we try hard to make them feel welcome and honored. We strive to demonstrate excellence in every respect, right down to the linen tablecloths and china for dinners. Each event depends heavily on the generosity of volunteers, friends from the community, or staff members who serve beyond their normal work hours.

In addition to conferences at our own facilities, Focus has staged large arena-style events around the country, most notably the Life on the Edge Tour for parents and teens and Renewing the Heart conferences for women. Many stories that emerge from these gatherings continue to inspire us.

One involved a couple named Elizabeth and Bill, who learned that their youngest son was desperately ill and would need a heart transplant to survive. Their physician arranged for the boy to be placed on a waiting list as an emergency case. Before long, they were told that a donor heart had become available. Though elated, Elizabeth and Bill were also deeply troubled that someone else had to lose a child in order for their son to live.

At the hospital, the doctor informed them of the tragedy that had given their little boy a second chance at life. Two sisters, alone at home, had gotten their father's gun down from a shelf to play with it. When the gun went off, one of the girls was killed. Her grief-stricken parents made the life-giving decision to donate their eight-year-old daughter's heart.

Elizabeth felt great compassion for the family who had given life to her son. So on Mother's Day, she asked to meet them. Still grieving, Sue, the girl's mother, placed her ear against the boy's chest and heard the heartbeat within. Elizabeth described it as "a holy moment."

Soon afterward, Elizabeth invited Sue to attend a Renewing the Heart conference, and she agreed to go. Moved by the messages and music, Sue realized her need for Christ and asked Jesus to be her Lord and Savior. In the anguish of her daughter's death, Sue had understood sacrifice and how life could come out of death. God used Elizabeth's love to bring Sue to Himself, so that she, too, could receive the gift of a new heart. ■

CONFERENCES

A Focus volunteer serves at a conference dinner.

Other volunteers help to sign in people as conference guests arrive on our campus.

Local volunteers are often recruited to help with sales at out-of-state events.

The first Focus over Fifty conference held at Focus headquarters in 1999.

A time of encouragement for pastors' wives.

Several large events are held on the Focus campus every year. Event staff and volunteers work together to make each one a positive experience for the attendees.

Our conferences always allow for times of fellowship.

Many ministries set up information booths at Focus events.

Young people attend Life on the Edge Tours with their parents, but have some teens-only sessions during the day.

"*When our youngest daughter, Megan, was in high school, we attended a Life on the Edge conference. I remember thinking, 'Do we really need this? Our girls are turning out so well.' But it was wonderful. The most awesome part was when Megan, her dad, and I stood, held hands, and prayed together! We promised that we'd see each other in heaven. It was a commitment that none of us will ever forget.*"

—CARLA O'CONNELL, CONSTITUENT

Miles McPherson speaks to teens and parents on the issue of purity.

Parents and teens are encouraged to discuss questions at various points in the sessions.

HIGHER LEARNING

As DR. DOBSON WAS WRITING *Life on the Edge*, he became deeply concerned about young people who were preparing to leave home and enter college. He asked the Focus staff to develop a program for students that would teach a Christian worldview and communicate a biblical model for the family.

In 1995, the ministry launched the Focus on the Family Institute (FFI), which provides an academic setting for young people to learn the importance of family and sharpen their Christian beliefs. In conjunction with the Christian College Consortium, FFI staff developed a curriculum that allows college students to gain academic credits as they study for a semester at our Colorado Springs campus. Institute students leave with a deeper understanding of the preeminence of evangelism, the permanence of marriage, the value of bearing and raising children, the sanctity of human life, and the relationship between church, family, and government.

Above, students grapple with important issues during lectures at the Institute.

Opposite: Institute students pack Dr. Dobson's office during a question-and-answer session.

Below, two of our early classes.

The program has grown from sixty-four students in our first year to our current enrollment of 264. More than 350 schools, both secular and Christian, have been represented at FFI, and over a hundred schools have agreements with the Institute. Students from numerous Christian denominations, home states, ethnic backgrounds (including twenty-five international students), academic majors, ages, and professional goals have benefited from the Institute's teachings. The Institute offers sixteen units of college credit for students in a wide variety of academic majors. In addition to classroom instruction, students participate in internships throughout the ministry, and

more than forty alumni have joined the Focus staff as employees.

Though most students come for the academic experience, many find their personal and spiritual lives changed as well.

"Students have talked with me and other staff about their struggles with pornography, eating disorders, broken family relationships, and other significant issues," says Dr. Michael Rosebush, vice president of the Focus on the Family Institute. "In each case, God uses the Focus setting as a safe harbor for these students to experience healing, deepen their faith, and explore their dreams. We keep in touch with many graduates. It's exciting to see how God used their time here to solidify their faith and move them to a place where He can utilize their talents and gifts."

Sometimes God uses the FFI experience to redirect students' lives. Andrew Kalitka came to the Institute as a psychology major who planned on a profession in counseling. As a result of his experience here, he pursued a new vocation and has published a nationally distributed photography book about God's beauty and purpose. Similarly, Jimmy Holbrook arrived desiring to become a youth pastor; four years later, he ran for Congress and is now a head pastor of a thriving church in Oklahoma.

"God has a reason for bringing each student to the Focus Institute," Dr. Rosebush says. "We're thrilled that He is using our staff and curricula to cause growth and change in the young men and women who study here." ∎

Time in class is balanced with opportunities to relax and discuss what the students have been learning.

"When I came to the Institute, I had decided to teach high school government. But through a practicum in Focus's Public Policy department I realized that instead of teaching about the importance of government, I could play a role within it! I am currently pursuing a Masters of Public Policy, and hope to develop and implement policy that will have a positive impact on the family. The Institute equipped me with the Christian leadership and knowledge I need to go out and impact the world for His glory." —ABBYLIN H. SELLERS, INSTITUTE STUDENT

MORE THAN HEAD KNOWLEDGE

Here is a sampling of courses offered
to Institute students:

Christian Worldview Studies
This course helps students better understand
the core presuppositions of the Christian worldview
and to contrast them with competing worldviews.
Students are taught to think critically about the
ultimate issues of human existence so they can
live more purposeful lives and participate
constructively in the larger sociocultural debate.

Family, Church, and Society Studies
This course encourages students to think about
the relationships between the family, the church,
and society—and it emphasizes the importance
of the church's role in helping families and
in influencing society.

Family Life Studies
Students are equipped with personal strategies
for promoting healthy families by specifically
focusing on parenting and the sanctity of human life.
Biblical teachings, existing research, and current
parenting techniques are reviewed with the goal
of helping students to develop strategies for
dealing with family problems and challenges.

Marriage and Leadership Studies
This course helps students to become leaders
who are passionate, persuasive, and respectful,
and it equips them with personal strategies for
promoting healthy families—beginning with their
own relationships. Students will be exposed to
typical problematic issues that most spouses
and leaders confront as they attempt to
establish healthy relationships.

Finding Hope in Tragedy

Dr. Dobson has long loved the game of basketball, and he played regularly with a group of staff members until his heart attack on August 15, 1990. A significant event in his life—and a landmark in Focus's history—took place on January 5, 1988, during one of these early-morning basketball games.

Pete Maravich, a former college and NBA star, was scheduled to record a *Focus* radio program later in the day, and he accepted an invitation to play in a pickup game before the taping. After playing for about forty-five minutes, everyone took a break, and Pete and Dr. Dobson had a chance to talk. During that brief conversation, Pete mentioned that although he had been experiencing increased pain in his shoulder over the previous few months, he hoped to get back into casual competition.

As their conversation concluded, Dr. Dobson asked, "So, Pete, how are you feeling today?"

He answered, "I feel great!" But as he turned to walk away, Pete suddenly collapsed to the floor.

"As I walked over to him, I realized he was having a seizure," Dr. Dobson recalls. "I began CPR, and the other players quickly came to assist. But within about twenty seconds, he was gone. 'Pistol Pete' Maravich, one of the world's greatest athletes, died there in my arms at forty years of age. The autopsy later revealed that he had a congenital malformation of his heart."

Pete Maravich knew Jesus Christ as his personal Savior, and he was ready to meet God. Nevertheless, Dr. Dobson was deeply shaken by what had occurred that day. When he returned home from the gym and the hospital, he sat down with his son, Ryan, who was seventeen years old at the time. Here's what Dr. Dobson told him:

> Ryan, I want you to understand what has happened here. Pete's death was not an unusual tragedy that has happened to only one man and his family. We must all face death sooner or later. No one will escape ultimately, and it will also happen to me. Without being morbid about it, I want you to begin to prepare yourself for that time.
>
> When it does happen, there is one thought I want to leave with you. I may not have the opportunity to give you my "last words" then, so let me express them to you right now. My message for you is, be there! Be there to meet your mother and me in heaven. This is the only thing of real significance in your life.

"Pistol Pete" Maravich, above, set a number of records on the court, but his faith was more important to him than his fame.

Opposite: Coaches taught more than just basketball skills at the camps. Many young people made commitments to Christ as a result of their influence and example.

"One particular broadcast that changed my life forever was Dr. Dobson's testimony of Pete Maravich. I was driving home from work, listening. I had been running from the Lord for several years after a terrible divorce. I was remarried and had three kids looking to me for guidance. Dr. Dobson got to the end of his story and shared how he went home to Ryan and said, 'No matter what, be there.' At that point, something just broke, and I began to sob. Years of callous running fell away, and God broke through. I have never been the same since. Thank you, Dr. Dobson. I will be there and so will my children." —Leslie Griffith, constituent

Not just for guys: A local newspaper article, top, spotlights one of the girls' camps.

Above, kids work on new skills during intense drills.

Coach and camp director Gary Lydic with Ray, at right.

That momentous event—along with similar experiences over the years—confirmed for Dr. Dobson and other leaders at Focus that this ministry's foremost purpose is to win people to Christ. That's why our mission statement reads: "Focus on the Family's primary reason for existence is to cooperate with the Holy Spirit in disseminating the Gospel of Jesus Christ to as many people as possible, and, specifically, to accomplish that objective by helping to preserve traditional values and the institution of the family."

Given this mission—and Focus's connection to the game of basketball—several staff members formulated an ambitious plan to offer basketball camps in cities around the country. The goal was to reach children—especially boys from single-parent homes—with the life-giving message that God loves them and has a divine purpose for their lives. The first camp took place in June 1988, just a few months after Pete Maravich's death.

Gary Lydic, coordinator of these camps, recalls a significant experience that took place at a camp in Atlanta. "A boy named Ray had enrolled in the program, but tragically, he suffered from a debilitating disease," Gary recalls. "Although he wanted to play, his physical condition simply wouldn't permit it. But Focus basketball camps were about more than athletics—they were about the eternal destinies of kids."

So Gary developed a plan to involve Ray, enlisting him to distribute juice to the other kids. "As the camp continued, those thirsty, exhausted kids began to look forward to seeing Ray's face," Gary says. "For them, 'Ray juice,' as they started to call it, became a symbol of refreshment and strength. And Ray became a kind of hero."

At the end of the camp, an awards ceremony was held. When Ray's name was called, the kids started chanting, "Ray! Ray! Ray!" Their shouts grew louder and louder as Ray struggled to the front of the gym. Before it was all over, the building was vibrating with the noise. "When all the other kids chanted his name, Ray smiled and cried at the same time," Gary recalls.

The camps continued for eight years, and more than 750 young people responded to the gospel message with either a first-time decision or a recommitment to follow Christ. In Gary's words, "That made it all worthwhile!" ∎

"When I heard that Focus's basketball camp was coming to San Diego, I wrote to ask if it were possible for my eight-year-old son to receive a scholarship. Focus sponsored Samuel—and he accepted Jesus Christ at that camp." —STEPHANIE WALLACE, CONSTITUENT

BIKE FOR THE FAMILY

Above, C. J. Palmer, a host for one of our affiliates in Anchorage, with his son in Alaska in July 2001.

Opposite: Florida riders give all the glory to God!

CALL IT "TOUR DE FOCUS." For eighteen months in 2001 and 2002, thousands of people took part in Focus's National Bike Ride for the Family, which rallied community support for family issues and introduced people to our various ministries. With the help of major sponsors such as lightsource.com, the promotional and ministry opportunity led up to the celebration of Focus on the Family's twenty-fifth anniversary in July 2002. The ride's organizers planned fifty state rides with thirty-five to forty-five cyclists participating in each.

Molly Saunders of Mount Vernon, Ohio, recalls the event's impact on her and her community: "Because I am diabetic and have an insulin pump, I was afraid I wouldn't be able to participate in the National Bike Ride for the Family. But I did, and God used me and others to bring about citywide revival in my town."

A group of pastors and church members had been praying that God would unite the Christians in Mount Vernon so they could work together to spread the Gospel. According to Molly, God used the cycling event to answer those prayers.

"God took my idea for a potluck dinner and changed it into the Ohio Family Fest, a day-long evangelistic event to welcome the riders to Mount Vernon on June 2, 2001. Two radio stations—a Christian one and a secular one—publicized the event. And when we asked a local printing company to donate a thousand promotional posters, they gave us ten thousand!"

Liz Pritchard and Molly Saunders rode through rain and hail before arriving at the Ohio Family Fest on day two of the ride, June 2001.

Despite the rainy weather, more than a thousand people attended the Ohio Family Fest and were treated to Christian entertainment, food, music, games, and gospel presentations. Twelve churches sold food to raise money for missions and ministry endeavors, and they gave ten percent of their money to Focus. A T-shirt company sold specially designed shirts and donated the proceeds to Focus.

"When we rode into Mount Vernon, soaking wet, we were greeted by cheers and thunderous applause," Molly says. "Then Brian Slivka, Tom Mason, and Ryan Dobson shared about the ministry of Focus on the Family with the crowd."

More than fifteen people began a relationship with Jesus Christ as a result of the event, and several thousand dollars were raised in support of Focus's ministry. But that was just the beginning. "The real miracle is what's happened since the bike ride," Molly explains. "We are seeing many churches growing, more people praying, and hundreds coming to know Jesus as Savior. I thank God for bringing Focus on the Family's National Bike Ride to stimulate revival in Mount Vernon." ■

"Focus on the Family is near and dear to my heart, and I jumped at the opportunity to be a part of the bike ride. I enjoy riding, but more than that, I wanted to go out and meet people. There are so many supporters of Focus who aren't able to travel to the ministry and meet the staff. The National Bike Ride for the Family allows us to give back to them and ask, 'How can we help you? How can we minister to you?' I have been blessed to hear many accounts of how Focus has ministered to people and made a difference in their lives." —RYAN DOBSON

NATIONAL BIKE RIDE FOR THE FAMILY

Participants at the South Carolina ride, May 2001.

Celebrating at the finish line in North Carolina, May 2001.

Alabama riders covered over two hundred miles for the family in March 2001.

Lunch at a roadside park during the Indiana ride, June 2001.

Riders in Florida, February 2001.

Dr. Dobson and dog "Freedom" with Ryan after the Virginia ride, April 2001. Ryan participated in nearly half the rides.

Riders in each state raised money for Focus and brought awareness for family issues. These photos represent more than two thousand riders who participated in over fifty rides—changing many lives as a result.

Alabama riders replenish themselves with food and water along the route.

Riders at the finish line in Michigan, after one of our longest rides, in June 2001.

National Bike Ride staff Ryan Dobson, Stephanie Mayabb, Brian Slivka, and Liz Pritchard in Alaska.

A victory cheer goes up as the riders approach the finish line on the Alaska ride, July 2001.

Riders pose before crossing over a historic covered bridge in Georgia, March 2001.

PART FIVE

GETTING THE WORD OUT

Creating Biblical Resources to Strengthen Families

"THIS IS WHAT WE SPEAK, NOT IN WORDS TAUGHT US BY HUMAN WISDOM BUT IN WORDS TAUGHT BY THE SPIRIT, EXPRESSING SPIRITUAL TRUTHS IN SPIRITUAL WORDS."

[1 CORINTHIANS 2:13]

Focus on the Family's mission statement says that we exist "to spread the Gospel by strengthening families." So how do we fulfill that mission? Primarily by providing an abundance of practical, biblically based resources families can use to address virtually any issue they encounter. Through radio broadcasts, magazines, books, videos, and other tools, we equip people of all ages to strengthen their family bonds and grow in their understanding of God.

Focus began twenty-five years ago with Dr. Dobson offering help to families through his books, audio tapes, video series, live speaking engagements, and radio. Before long, we began providing updates to our extended family through newsletters. As Focus continued to grow, the newsletter evolved into a magazine, and we added a monthly letter from Dr. Dobson as well. Through the years, new publications were added to communicate our family message to other audiences.

Eventually, we ventured into book publishing so we could offer a fuller treatment of some stories that were first told on the broadcast. In time, this effort grew to include a wide range of books addressing topics to equip husbands and wives, moms and dads, children and teens with biblical principles for everyday living.

Videos have provided a versatile medium for presenting biblical messages in fresh new ways. We've produced animated stories for young children, live action for older kids, topical videos to get teens' attention, and faith lessons for the whole family. Some of these resources have also been edited for use in secular classrooms as well as for television specials, and the response has been astounding.

A recent emphasis has been Heritage Builders, an effort that provides materials for parents to help pass down their faith from one generation to the next. We've also begun taking advantage of opportunities on the Internet by producing a webzine for college students as well as numerous websites that support other areas of Focus's ministry.

The Focus on the Family film crew on location near Pergamum, in western Turkey, while filming *That the World May Know.*

PERIODICALS WITH PURPOSE

AFTER TWENTY-FIVE YEARS OF MINISTRY, with numerous glossy magazines published each month, our early publication efforts seem quite humble!

Not long after Dr. Dobson established Focus, we began producing a two-color, four-page newsletter that was sent to anyone who requested it. It featured—as it still does—inspirational articles and practical advice as well as news about Focus and the broadcast schedule. After a few design changes, this modest publication was transformed into a four-color, sixteen-page monthly periodical in 1983—the first of many design metamorphoses over the years. Meanwhile, Dr. Dobson retained the newsletter format for his own commentaries, a monthly feature he continues to create to this day.

As time passed, it became increasingly apparent that Focus's many friends and supporters included a wide variety of ages, backgrounds, and perspectives. To effectively minister to these diverse groups, we created targeted publications. Eventually we found ourselves producing a whole spectrum of magazines, each one specifically designed to address the unique concerns of a particular readership, such as parents, kids, teens, and Christian professionals.

The first of these spin-off periodicals was *Focus on the Family Clubhouse*, a magazine devoted to children between the ages of eight and twelve. *Clubhouse*, along with the newly launched *Adventures in Odyssey* broadcast, was part of a push in the mid-1980s to offer kids wholesome, faith-affirming entertainment and educational materials. *Clubhouse* was soon followed by *Clubhouse Jr.*, which is geared toward younger children, ages four to eight. Later, as *Clubhouse* fans themselves began moving into the adolescent years, our periodicals staff created two new teen magazines: *Brio*, for girls, and *Breakaway*, for boys.

In the years that followed, we launched several other magazines that addressed the unique needs of select groups, including *Physician*, *Teachers in Focus*, *Pastor's Family*, *Single-*

"I don't think I will ever forget the overwhelming sense of gratitude I felt for Single-Parent Family *magazine. My single-parent friends and I felt so loved and included in the family of God (finally!). I still have every copy of that magazine that I received. I used information from the publication to write a research paper on single parents and prepare a presentation on single parenting for our church. My children even enjoyed reading many of the articles. I now receive* Plugged In, *which they also enjoy reading!"* —ANN LANGSTON-DYKES, CONSTITUENT

Parent Family, and *LifeWise* (for mature adults). In the late 1990s, however, Focus leadership decided to cease publication of *Teachers in Focus*, *Pastor's Family*, and *Single-Parent Family* as stand-alone periodicals. (The latter two groups now receive specialized versions of our flagship magazine, *Focus on the Family*, instead.)

Apart from these targeted magazines stands *Citizen*, a periodical Focus launched in the late 1980s in order to highlight public policy issues that impacted the family and traditional values.

In addition to publishing eight print magazines, we offer resources in different formats. *Boundless*, geared for college students, is a webzine available only on the Internet. And our Youth Culture department produces *Plugged In* (formerly *Parental Guidance*), a monthly newsletter that includes commentary on youth culture and reviews of movies, music, and TV shows. To provide up-to-the-minute information to this readership, we've created pluggedinmag.com, which is consistently one of the most visited areas on Focus's web site.

Our goal from the beginning has been to produce high-quality publications that offer readers both inspirational and helpful information—all wrapped in an attractive package. The dozens of awards our magazines have won—and the thousands of encouraging letters we've received—assure us that we've met the challenge. ∎

A 1987 photo of Ray Seldomridge, at left, the first editor of *Clubhouse* and *Clubhouse Jr.*, and Tim Jones, senior art director of periodicals, in Arcadia, California.

The current magazine, top, features several targeted segments that contain different content depending on the constituent's family needs.

BOUNDLESS TRUTH

By now, many Focus constituents know what a webzine is. But in 1998, when *Boundless* was launched, "webzine" was a new word that conveyed a whole new way of reaching an audience.

One of our Focus board members, whose son was in college, noticed the gap in resources to equip young adults for the road ahead. "After *Clubhouse Jr.*, *Clubhouse*, and *Breakaway* and *Brio*, then what?" he asked. So he donated the means to launch *Boundless*, an Internet magazine for college students.

We chose the name *Boundless* because it describes our new "unbound" electronic publication, but also because it reflects the full and abundant life God offers young adults through His boundless love. College can be a rough time for young people. Truth and high moral standards hold little value on many campuses, and universities are often a breeding ground for a worldview that's hostile to Christianity. We wanted to offer students an alternative—one filled with hope.

Boundless equips students to articulate and model moral truths to their fellow collegians as well as to their professors. With thought-provoking articles by some of the top Christian thinkers, *Boundless* offers wisdom about the issues that matter most as students navigate the classroom and then life beyond college.

Our Magazines

"It's so nice to receive Christian material that relates directly to my life. Time and time again, when I've struggled over an issue, Brio has addressed it from an open, honest, totally-God perspective. You've provoked thoughts, at times arguments, that challenge my beliefs. I really really really am thankful to all of you. You've changed my life. Thanks a bunch for yielding to the Spirit and impacting thousands of teenage-girls' lives!"

— NADINE K. WOLF, CONSTITUENT

The first Focus on the Family *magazine, no longer in newsletter format, July 1983.*

Clubhouse, *for children ages eight through twelve, began in February 1987.*

Citizen *debuted in November 1987.*

Clubhouse Jr. *began in January 1988 for children ages four through eight.*

The first issue of Physician, *for medical professionals, January 1989.*

The ever-popular Brio *was started in March 1990 for teen girls.*

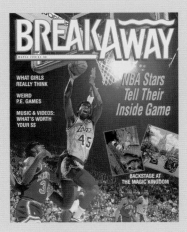

Breakaway *for teen guys also began in March 1990.*

Originally Parental Guidance *(July 1990), this newsletter was renamed* Plugged In *in January 1996.*

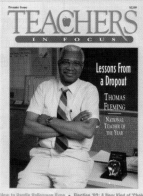

Teachers in Focus *debuted in October 1992 and ended in December 2000.*

In October 1994, Single-Parent Family *was launched. Its run ended in December 2000, and it is now a specialized version of* Focus on the Family.

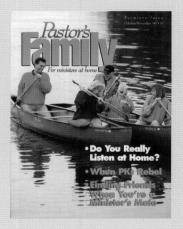

Pastor's Family *started in October 1996 and ended in December 1998. It is now a specialized version of* Focus on the Family.

For the over-fifty audience, we began LifeWise *in September 1999.*

We've produced hundreds of magazines over the years, and continue to be touched by the mail we receive from readers who have been helped by these efforts. Pictured are the premiere issues of each periodical.

Brio & Beyond *was started in September 2001 for older teen girls.*

Join the Club!

Both *Clubhouse* and *Clubhouse Jr.* offer great ideas for projects that parents and children can work on together.

Below, some recent issues of *Clubhouse* and *Clubhouse Jr.* magazines for young children.

RAISING GODLY, RESPONSIBLE CHILDREN has never been easy, but the permissive culture in which we live makes the task all the more difficult. That's why Focus has, from the very beginning, sought to assist and encourage parents who endeavor to raise kids with strong morals and biblical values.

In 1987, the ministry launched *Clubhouse* magazine for children ages eight to twelve. This publication is Focus's longest-running resource for children—even older than *Adventures in Odyssey*, which began airing nine months after the first issue of *Clubhouse* rolled off the presses. While the publication today looks drastically different from the original eight-page version, its goal has remained the same: to provide family-oriented stories, games, and activities that offer good, clean fun and reinforce Christian values. Over the years, *Clubhouse* has grown to twenty-four pages and is now read by more than 115,000 kids in thirty-five countries.

Letters like the following, from an eight-year-old boy in England, inspire us to continue publishing magazines that are both thought-provoking and engaging:

Dear *Clubhouse*,

I love *Clubhouse*. My best friend is Timmy. He is a Christian. His family told us about *Adventures in Odyssey* and *Clubhouse*. They also told us about Jesus. In November I asked Jesus into my life. God be with you.

Love, Ollie

Here's more encouraging news: In a recent survey sent to parents of *Clubhouse* readers, over eight percent indicated that the magazine had been influential in their children accepting Jesus Christ as their personal Savior. That means the magazine has helped nearly ten thousand current readers make a decision to follow Jesus—and that doesn't take into account the thousands of kids who have outgrown *Clubhouse* through the years!

Of course, we're equally concerned about younger readers. So, just eleven months after the first issue of *Clubhouse* arrived in mailboxes, *Clubhouse Jr.* was launched for four- to eight-year-olds. Like its older sibling, *Clubhouse Jr.* strives to help parents raise their children with godly values.

Readership for this publication has grown from sixty-seven thousand the first year to over ninety thousand currently. One parent recently commented: "I know I can trust Focus on the Family. I can go through *Clubhouse Jr.* with my daughter or allow her to read it alone without concern for negative or false content." ■

"I recently attended a revival at my church and was totally changed. I returned home, craving some guidance. That's when I stumbled upon an issue of Breakaway. A testimony I read about in the magazine encouraged me to take my faith to a deeper, more radical level. I'm praying for the kind of strength I need so I can stand up for my God!" —S.H., CONSTITUENT

TEEN SPIRIT

MOST MESSAGES TEENAGERS RECEIVE from the media today are anything but uplifting and wholesome. For more than a decade, Focus has been offering a positive alternative.

The first issue of *Brio* magazine for teen girls arrived in mailboxes in March 1990, with contemporary Christian artist Michael W. Smith gracing the cover. The response was immediate, and circulation grew quickly.

But the magazine delves into more than just music and popular culture. Ministry is also a focus. "I love to run articles that prompt readers to act," says Susie Shellenberger, who has held the editorial reins since the magazine's inception. "*Brio* girls have responded to stories about children in need and have proven their tender hearts by sponsoring more than three thousand children through Compassion International." More than twelve hundred readers have also participated in missions through *Brio*'s annual two-week international missions program to Third World countries.

Susie says the purpose of *Brio* is threefold: first, to lead teen girls into an intimate, growing relationship with Jesus Christ; second, to guide them toward a confident, positive self-image; and finally, to help them establish healthy relationships.

"I'll never forget the cover story we did on seventeen-year-old Charity Allen from Southern California," Susie recalls. "She was cast as a new female lead in the soap opera *Days of Our Lives* but turned down the fame, money, and career opportunity when she realized she'd be compromising her relationship with Christ."

Susie says the magazine tries to feature such role models—actresses, models, musicians, and athletes whom readers can look up to. "But my favorite stories are the ones that highlight ordinary teen girls who are living extraordinary lives," Susie says. "These girls are doing incredible things and making wise decisions because of the supernatural power of God saturating their lives."

Brio's counterpart for teen guys, *Breakaway*, began publication at the same time, with an initial readership of 15,654. Today, the magazine reaches more than 100,000 boys throughout the world. The first issue featured NBA great A. C. Green, who delivered a strong message about sexual abstinence. Through the years, other Christian role models have found a place in *Breakaway*: David Robinson, Kurt Warner, Michael W. Smith, and Frank Peretti, not to mention countless missionaries and ordinary men who are doing great things for God.

"I consider my work as editor a mission," says Michael Ross, "and I view *Breakaway* as much more than type on pages. This magazine goes deep into the lives of readers, guiding their steps, building their confidence, and leading them into a stronger relationship with Jesus Christ."

When speaking of his readers, Michael likes to quote a line from the book *Wild at Heart* by John Eldredge: "'Simply look at the dreams and desires written in the heart of every boy: to be a hero, to be a warrior, to live a life of adventure.' That's *Breakaway*'s mission—launching boys into the adventure of manhood." ∎

Brio and *Breakaway* magazines for teens were started with funds donated by a concerned parent. *Brio & Beyond* is a recent addition for older girls. The three magazines currently reach about 300,000 teens each month and continue to grow.

Teens find help and encouragement for Christian living in the pages of *Brio* and *Breakaway*.

FAMILY NEWS FROM FOCUS

FROM THE VERY BEGINNING, Dr. Dobson has made it a high priority to have open communication with friends of the ministry. His monthly newsletter, currently distributed under the title *Family News from Dr. James Dobson*, was Focus on the Family's earliest vehicle for staying in touch with supporters. It has remained a constant and reliable feature of this ministry throughout our two-and-a-half-decade history. Readership has now passed the two million mark.

Early on, the newsletter became Dr. Dobson's "personal responsibility" in a very important sense. In the midst of everything else going on at Focus, he has come to view the penning of this monthly message as a unique opportunity to maintain a direct link with the people we seek to serve.

"I take it very, very seriously," he says. "All month long, I weigh what the Lord would have me say about the family in that letter. I'm keenly aware that it may have a broader impact than anything I'm able to communicate over the radio."

The newsletter has also been significant by reason of its versatility. With the cooperation of nearly thirty assistants, researchers, and fact-checkers, Dr. Dobson has used it to address everything from crucial issues (Supreme Court decisions) to lighthearted musings (the respective merits of dogs and cats as pets). Sometimes it's a platform from which to "sound the alarm"—to ask for help in heading off another cultural assault on traditional values. On other occasions, it's a forum for discussing marriage and parenting concerns. At still other times—in moments of acute need—it has been a way of letting our friends know about the ministry's financial challenges.

Paul Nelson, who served as Focus's executive vice president and chief financial officer from 1985 to 1994, recalls a significant incident involving the newsletter. He had just joined Focus after spending twenty-three years in the chemical and oil industries, and he was trying to figure out how a nonprofit ministry operates.

"I quickly realized we needed to establish a budgeting and estimating process," he says. "Not much time had been devoted to forecasting financial results because the ministry was growing rapidly and the mind-set was 'Move ahead, and the money will follow.'"

But in March of 1985, Focus's income leveled off at a time when expenses were climbing rapidly. Paul estimated that projections for the following three summer months were going to send the expense line above the income line. Cash reserves were pretty modest.

"I approached Dr. Dobson carefully, recognizing that we had not yet become comfortable with one another's styles since I had only been at Focus for three months," he recalls. "He received the information with serious concern. Our meeting precipitated a newsletter from him candidly explaining the financial squeeze the ministry was facing."

The Focus newsletter in April 1985 expressed Dr. Dobson's concerns about the financial needs of the ministry.

The letter produced an enormous response—by far the largest increase in giving Focus had ever received. Paul was delighted, yet somewhat bewildered, by the quick and generous response. He says he had not yet learned how wonderful the Christian public can be when a need is presented clearly and respectfully, especially when a ministry rarely asks for help.

One month later it was time to write the next newsletter. Dr. Dobson prepared a gracious thank-you letter that said the financial squeeze had ended due to the response of supporters. Paul loved the letter, but again became a bit concerned.

> I spoke with Rolf Zettersten, my colleague in the Focus cabinet, and we agreed that such a letter might unravel all the good results that had just been accomplished. Together we visited Dr. Dobson, and I said, "Jim, I know I have been here only a short time, but it seems to me that this letter is likely to cause donors to skip a contribution to Focus on the Family for that month since we are, in effect, telling them that our finances are just fine." I will never forget his answer. It was in a private setting with only the three of us, no outsider to impress. He said, "I have been concerned about the response from last month. There were some big checks in the mail. Some of them probably were tithe checks that belonged in the local church. Others might have normally been designated for another ministry, who this month might be hurting. I hear what you are saying, but I want to leave the letter just as it is written."
>
> Following the meeting, as I headed down the hallway to my office, I remember thinking, "I can work with this man. I can learn from him." And I did—for nine years!

Paul adds this postscript to the story: "The newsletter went out and the response from the Focus constituency did not suffer a decline, as I feared it might. I later saw a basic principle confirmed over and over again as God supplied the need of the ministry with just enough during each tough period. I believe an attitude of sincerely trusting the Lord while being straight with the ministry's donors enabled the organization to grow by nearly tenfold during the time that I was privileged to serve in leadership." ∎

May 29, 1985

Dear Friend:

Several weeks ago I made a radio announcement regarding the financial needs we are experiencing here at Focus on the Family. A few days later, I confirmed our difficult situation by sharing the details with our friends in my monthly letter. It was the first time I had been that candid about our circumstances in the eight-year history of Focus on the Family, and for good reason. When we came to the end of March and calculated income versus expenses, we had sustained a deficit of $466,000. It was recognized in an executive staff meeting that we could not survive for more than a few months if the trend continued, particularly in view of our unwillingness to spend more money than we are given.

But what wonderful people you are! We received an immediate outpouring of letters and phone calls from our friends and supporters across North America. When your gifts were combined with our efforts to reduce expenses, the deficit during the month of April was only $51,000 instead of $305,000 as anticipated. Although it is still too early to know the "bottom line" for May, we hope to end the month in the black. We still face a challenge to deal with the lean summer months, but we are extremely grateful for those who are standing with us financially during this difficult time.

Much more importantly, however, is the volume of prayer that has been expressed on our behalf. So many of you wrote to say that you were praying for us. What a beautiful experience it is to know that across the United States and Canada, people whom we have never met are speaking our names in their private moments before the Lord, asking Him to guide and sustain us in this time of need. And He has been quietly answering those petitions and assuring us of His care.

May I now ask in love, what are your needs today? Certainly, I am not the only member of the human family to go through valleys. Earlier this morning, I received a phone call from Judy Standridge, a guest on our broadcast in February. Three weeks ago, her 17-year-old daughter tragically overdosed on cocaine and another substance called a "designer drug" . . . a new

P.O. Box 500, Arcadia, CA 91006

The May 1985 letter simply thanked people for responding to the needs the prior month. Focus trusts the Lord to bring in what we need in order to do His work here.

At far left, Paul Nelson, former executive vice president of Focus on the Family, addresses staff at a Focus chapel.

Family dog Mindy, left, was the topic of a Focus newsletter in the late 1980s that addressed the issue of loneliness.

THE GIFT OF LIFE

THE DIAGNOSIS OF DOWN'S SYNDROME came in 1994, twenty weeks into Lynn Chittenden's pregnancy with her second child. It was the darkest time of her life.

"I tried to wish it away, talk it away, scream it away, and have friends pray it away," Lynn recalls. "But I knew that as a Christian, I could do nothing but accept this assignment, this role of mothering a special needs child. Honestly, I did it kicking and screaming. I did not want this baby and could not even pray for this baby other than uttering 'God, please make him normal.'"

Several months into her pregnancy, a friend sent her a copy of the December 1993 Focus Christmas newsletter, which told the story of an obstetrician, Frederic Loomis, who debated delivering a baby girl he knew would be born with only one leg. Reluctantly, Dr. Loomis decided not to abort the infant—and the family was crushed to find out their child was disabled. For almost two decades Dr. Loomis was burdened by guilt, feeling he should have aborted the girl to spare her parents such pain. Then one night he had a chance meeting with the family: The girl he'd once debated aborting had turned into a beautiful and accomplished musician! And her mother was glowing with pride.

The story served to be a powerful testimony to Lynn. "After I read the letter, I realized it doesn't matter what's wrong with David—God can work with anything!"

She put the fate and future of her child into God's care, tenaciously clinging to Proverbs 3:5: "Trust in the Lord with all your heart and lean not on your own understanding."

Lynn recalls, "My husband, Tom, and I named him David, which means 'beloved' in Hebrew. Through my pain, God showed me glimpses of His grace: My dear friend Jane said, 'Well done, thou good and faithful servant.' Another mom with a Down's syndrome child told me, 'No, you don't understand; we're the lucky ones.' My obstetrician said, 'You know, he'll never drink or do drugs or run with a bad crowd.'"

Lynn came to realize they were right. "More than anyone else," she says, "David demonstrates to me the meaning of God's love. The boy has an uncanny sense of who needs a smile or hug. Otherwise tough and surly people melt when he runs and throws his little arms around them."

One day while Lynn and David were in a bread store, he approached a young woman.

"Hi!" he said, flashing a big smile.

Almost in tears, she said, "Oh, I needed a friend today."

Since David has learned to pray at mealtimes, he has stretched the patience of Dad, Mom, and his brother, Tommy. Many of their meals and even snacks are interrupted by lengthy prayer sessions. And at bedtime, he prays for family, friends, teachers, and neighbors—virtually every one of them, past and present.

"Every human life—including those the world deems imperfect—has utmost value and worth," affirms Lynn. "Focus's newsletter, written so long ago, reminded me that, as Dr. Dobson said, 'Our obligation is to trust Him even when the pieces don't fit.'

"David is a gift to our family and community. He is teaching us the meaning of forgiveness, trust, and unconditional love. Those who have been fortunate enough to know a special needs child understand this: We're the lucky ones." ∎

Family physicians deliver both good and bad news to parents in the course of their work. Focus often helps and encourages families who have received troubling news about their child's health.

Opposite (left to right): Lynn, Tommy, David, and Tom Chittenden.

BOOK-MARKED FOR EXCELLENCE

Focus on the Family was honored with an Impact Award, above, for its sales booth at the Christian Bookseller's Association (pictured at top) in 2001.

Opposite: Young visitors to our bookstore enjoy the selection of children's books published by Focus and others.

IN 1986, AFTER NINE YEARS of producing broadcasts, newsletters, and magazines, Focus was well established as a communications ministry. The next step was to explore new ways we could support families with helpful, encouraging resources. The result? A venture into book publishing that began small (one book the first year) and grew into a full-fledged operation.

Early publications expanded the messages of popular radio guests, since more detailed information could be included in a book format. Some of the first books to display the Focus imprimatur were *Twice Pardoned* and its sequel, *Beyond the Barriers*, which told the story of ex-con Harold Morris; *Answers to Your Family's Financial Questions*, written by financial adviser Larry Burkett; *Language of Love*, a book about communication authored by Gary Smalley and John Trent; *Drug-Proof Your Kids*, a guidebook for parents by Steve Arterburn and Ken Burns; *The Debt Squeeze*, a book by Ron Blue that offers practical help to couples struggling with finances; and *God Uses Cracked Pots* and *Normal Is Just a Setting on Your Dryer*, which brought readers laughs and inspiration from Patsy Clairmont.

When our ministry vision expanded to include children, Focus on the Family Publishing created books for young readers: Cottontale Books by Pamela Kennedy for preschoolers; Psalty books created with Maranatha! for Kids, featuring characters created by Ernie and Debby Rettino; and three books by Ann Hibbard about G. T. and the Halo Express. The first books in the Adventures in Odyssey book series were also created to complement the radio series.

As our publishing venture expanded, so did the ages we sought to reach. In the late 1980s, we began developing series for juvenile and teen readers, including the Christy Miller and Sierra Jensen series by Robin Jones Gunn; the China Tate series by Lissa Halls Johnson; the Ladd Family Adventure books by Lee Roddy; the Daring Adventure series by Peter Reese Doyle; the Christian Heritage series by Nancy Rue; and the Passages series by Paul McCusker.

Over the years, some well-known authors have created resources for Focus on the Family, such as *Prodigals and Those Who Love Them* by Ruth Graham; *Finding the Love of Your Life* by Neil Clark Warren; *Bringing Up Kids Without Tearing Them Down* by Kevin Leman; and *Breakthrough Parenting* by John Maxwell. We've published numerous books to help couples strengthen their marriages as well: *The Marriage Masterpiece* by Al Janssen, *Always* by Betsy Holt and Mike Yorkey, and *It Takes Two to Tango* by Gary and Norma Smalley. Many books have also offered help to parents raising children: *Creative Correction* by Lisa Whelchel Cauble, *The Way They Learn* by Cynthia Tobias, and *FaithTraining* by Joe White, to name just a few.

We believe God has called us to encourage families with His messages of love and life. That call drives our creative vision. In the last few years, Focus on the Family Publishing has partnered with Tyndale House Publishers, Tommy Nelson, Bethany House, Zondervan, and other publishers to get our family resources out to as many homes as possible. And we continue to work with our own staff of writers as well as many other authors to create resources that will strengthen marriages, encourage parents, and bring youths into a closer walk with our Lord. ■

Heritage Builders

Most Christian parents want desperately to pass down their faith to their children. But how can they do it in a way that's both effective and engaging? That very question led to the development of Heritage Builders, a series of resources that helps parents be intentional about teaching spiritual truths to their kids.

Kurt Bruner, one of the founders of Heritage Builders and Focus on the Family's vice president of resource development, explains:

> The overwhelming majority of those who become Christians do so as children, yet many kids raised in a Christian home fail to make the faith their own by the time they reach adulthood. I felt the weight of the responsibility God had laid upon my shoulders by entrusting these young lives to my care. I also knew God would hold me accountable for my kids' spiritual development. But despite my seminary degree, despite the fact that I was an elder in my local church, despite being a staff member at Focus on the Family, I was doing absolutely nothing intentional about my own kids' spiritual training. I didn't want to bore them as I had been bored.
>
> About that time, in 1995, two other dads and I decided that it was time to come up with a new plan for motivating and equipping parents to pass a strong spiritual heritage to our children. We began experimenting at home with some fun and creative ways of teaching the faith, and we were pleased with the results. We wrote up some of our ideas, put them into book form, and began looking for opportunities to share our experiences with churches and parenting groups.

That ministry became Heritage Builders, which eventually became part of Focus on the Family. The earliest resources were the Family Night Tool Chests, which cover topics from basic Christian beliefs and characteristics to science and money matters. These books give parents all the guidance they need for creating fun and meaningful lessons for their families.

Buoyed by the positive response to the Tool Chest books, Focus decided to provide more faith-building resources. This led to the creation of the *Parents' Guide to the Spiritual*

At left, Olivia Bruner and her sons, Shaun, Kyle, and Troy, enjoy a Family Night activity together. Dad Kurt helped with the lesson after taking the picture.

Opposite: Some families spend time setting goals and making sure their upcoming Family Nights are on the calendar.

Below, two of the many Heritage Builders books, created to help parents pass their faith to young children and to teens.

"We often use the Heritage Builders Family Night ideas. It's the best thing that we have ever done to teach our children about God. They love Family Night and they verbally associate it with learning about God." —Sheila Hyde, constituent

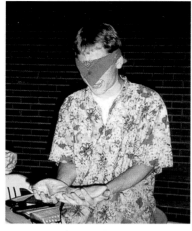

Josh Weidmann, above, gets a Family Night lesson about the power of the tongue that makes a lasting impression! (That's real tongue, too!)

Heritage Builders resources, seen opposite, equip parents with tools to take advantage of teachable moments in order to build a foundation of faith.

Growth of Children, a comprehensive book that helps moms and dads develop a plan for spiritual training that's tailored to the various ages and stages of their children and their family situation.

Next, we created a group of tools that help parents maximize teachable moments throughout the day and week. *Mealtime Moments* gives questions, object lessons, verses, and prayers to make even the family's time at the kitchen table a fun learning experience for children. *Joy Ride* provides games, discussion ideas, and Bible challenges that can be done in the car, whether on a trip to the grocery store or a family-vacation road trip. *Bedtime Blessings* features stories, activities, and a special prayer to make the last moments of the day special.

Heritage Builders has also created devotional books for school-age children, such as *My Time with God* and a series called KidWitness Tales, which follow fictional kids through real events from the Bible. All of these books, and many others, have been created to help get kids excited about reading the Bible and getting to know God better while they are young.

For moms and dads with older kids, the *Parents' Guide to the Spiritual Mentoring of Teens* assists with the often-difficult task of building the faith of their children through the adolescent years. It provides proven tactics for helping ignite teens' passion to be wholehearted disciples.

Additional Heritage Builders conferences, books, audiotapes, and resources are planned to encourage and equip parents. "Through the materials we've produced and the seminars we've organized," says Kurt Bruner, "thousands of moms and dads have moved beyond boring, awkward, or nonexistent spiritual discussions with their kids toward active and engaging lessons in spiritual growth. Like me, they've discovered that God does not call parents to complacency, but to intentional creativity!" ■

"I attended a Heritage Builders conference a year ago. It was wonderful. Because of what I heard at the conference, my family now spends almost every evening playing together, even if only for twenty minutes. We go out to eat less and instead try to come up with cool family things to do together. Each day, we talk to our kids about the ways in which God has provided for us, whether a bill was less than expected or someone offered to baby-sit for free. Because of the conference, we have tried to be deliberate in teaching our children our Christian values. It changed my life and the lives of my children." —JULIE BOWLICK, CONSTITUENT

JOINING FORCES

FOCUS HAS BEEN PRIVILEGED OVER THE YEARS to join forces with other ministries whose mission aligns with our own. One such fruitful relationship has been with Promise Keepers (PK), an organization that equips men to fulfill their responsibilities as Christian husbands, fathers, church members, and workers. As this ministry began to experience dramatic growth in the mid-1990s and the need for companion resources became apparent, Focus's Book Publishing department worked closely with PK to create books and study guides.

The first book, *Seven Promises of a Promise Keeper*, was published in 1994 and includes contributions from such leaders as Dr. Bill Bright, Dr. Dobson, Dr. Tony Evans, Bill McCartney, and Luis Palau. Given to every man who attended conferences that year, it captures the core of the Promise Keepers message, calling on men to live with integrity toward God, family, church, and the world. Hundreds of thousands of copies have since been distributed.

Subsequent books included *The Power of a Promise Kept* (1995), which features stories of men living out their promises; *Go the Distance* (1996), which includes chapters from Charles Colson, Jack Hayford, John Perkins, and others to help men put their commitment to Christ into action; and *The Making of a Godly Man Workbook* (1997), which guides men in developing a step-by-step plan for a lifetime of promise keeping.

Many husbands and dads heard about Promise Keepers (PK) for the first time through Focus broadcasts. Focus partnered with PK to create several books to help men put their promises to work.

Part of the Promise Keepers mission is to involve men in small Bible study groups for mutual encouragement and accountability. To help facilitate that goal, a series of small-group study guides was launched under the name Promise Builders. Focus aided in getting this series off the ground by publishing the second and third volumes, *Applying the Seven Promises* and *The Promise Keeper at Work*, extending their impact far beyond Promise Keepers' own distribution.

The years of being part of Promise Keepers' early growth were perhaps our most exciting period in publishing. God has used that ministry to draw untold thousands of men to Himself— and He has done so, in part, through many of the PK resources Focus has been able to provide. ∎

"As young parents, we began to greatly appreciate the books, tapes, films, and other resources for families produced by Focus on the Family. The ministry's efforts make parents aware of both the problems and the possibilities of raising Christian children in our secular culture. Now, as grandparents, we are doubly grateful to God for the expanded ministry that benefits many more families." —REVEREND ART AND BETH DOMINY, CONSTITUENTS

FOCUS ON FILMS

ABOUT THE SAME TIME FOCUS BEGAN PUBLISHING books, we also started producing videos. The first film, *Twice Pardoned,* featuring ex-con Harold Morris, became a powerful message to teens when it was released in 1987. A year later, many lives were touched when Mike Adkins told the story of his neighbor in *A Man Called Norman.* Teachers, parents, and students were inspired by Guy Doud's films *Molder of Dreams* (1989) and *Teacher of the Year* (1990). And Dr. Dobson presented a challenging message about pornography in *A Winnable War* (1987).

Building on the success of those early efforts, Focus on the Family Films has grown tremendously over the years. We partnered with Tyndale House Publishers in the creation of the popular *McGee and Me* videos for children, and later we created the action-packed *Last Chance Detectives.* The popular radio series *Adventures in Odyssey* inspired a series of animated videos for younger children as well. All of these series were created to pass biblical values to children through the stories portrayed.

To complement ministry efforts in the early 1990s aimed at encouraging abstinence among teens, Focus created a little video called *Sex, Lies, and ... the Truth.* Hosted by Kirk Cameron and Chelsea Noble, this film featured several well-known athletes, actors, and popular speakers. No one had any idea how God was going to multiply the impact of this program. An edited version was created for public schools, and thousands of junior high and high schools purchased it for classroom use. We began getting feedback from parents, teachers, students, and administrators saying the video made teens question the so-called "safe sex" message they were being taught. As a result, thousands made commitments to wait until marriage.

Above, actors help illustrate Guy Doud's classroom story in *Molder of Dreams*, 1989, pictured below with one of the Christian video awards it won.

Opposite: The *Last Chance Detectives* actors pose for a cover photo during a film shoot in Kingman, Arizona.

"We have five children under the age of eight, and our three oldest ones have grown up with your videos. The videos by Focus on the Family are often the only material we can put on our television and safely walk away from, knowing that our kids will not be shown anything they shouldn't be seeing. Most important, they love the stories—and we do, too. My wife and I love following the exploits of the Odyssey gang, McGee, and the Last Chance Detectives."

—THOMAS ROBEY, CONSTITUENT

Updating a Classic

In the summer of 2000, Focus on the Family board members asked, What would Dr. Dobson's original film series, which reached an estimated fifteen million people around the globe, look like in the twenty-first century? Could Focus have that kind of impact on a new generation of parents?

Creative minds from throughout the ministry met to brainstorm ways in which those timeless parenting principles might be presented to today's moms and dads. Prototypes took shape. Dr. Dobson, whose books and TV commentaries would form the foundation of the project, gave input and approval. Soon we began writing scripts, attempting to distill more than a quarter century of child-rearing wisdom into four dozen fast-paced video segments.

Our film team crisscrossed the country, interviewing parents and kids to learn their concerns and opinions about family life. Some of America's most experienced animators, who had worked on TV series and movies such as *Space Jam* and *The Iron Giant*, crafted cartoon sequences that would deliver key points in a funny, memorable way. And at the heart of it all are shared stories and straight talk about how today's families work—and how they're meant to work.

Thus was born *Your Child*, a comprehensive video series that tackles topics vital to twenty-first-century parents—discipline, self-confidence, education, guarding children in a dangerous world, bringing up boys, surviving the teen years, and much more. An engaging, easy-to-use curriculum guide supplements the video, helping participants in churches, small groups, and elsewhere apply the advice to their own unique families. A 2003 release is anticipated.

A year or so later, we commissioned a Spanish translation of the video and curriculum to further the reach of the message, and God has taken that resource into homes and schools far beyond our borders. After several years, another abstinence video, *No Apologies*, was created with a more current look.

Through the years, other teen resources have been created that deal with absolute truth versus relativism (*My Truth, Your Truth, Whose Truth?*), the importance of discernment in music and video choices (*Mind Over Media*), and the deadly impact of drugs (*Masquerade*). We've also produced a seven-video set based on Dr. Dobson's book *Life on the Edge*, which features discussions on finding God's will, the keys to lifelong love, the dangers of pornography, and sexual purity.

When Dr. and Shirley Dobson heard Michigan Bible instructor Ray Vander Laan's powerful teaching in Israel, they wanted to share that experience with others in our Focus audience. With a generous gift from Ed and Elsa Prince, we produced a series of videos and leaders' guides to teach the same faith lessons to many hundreds of families. Over several years of production, we created five sets of lessons that became the series *That the World May Know*.

Some of our more current projects include a computer-animated video series called *Ribbits*, which communicates biblical values to young children, and *Your Child*, a multi-set parenting curriculum that includes animation, man-on-the-street interviews, lessons from Dr. Dobson, and topics ranging from toddler to teen issues.

It's been said that God will use any means to reach people with the message of His love and compassion. At Focus, we're certainly seeing Him use the relatively modern—and enormously popular—medium of film to spread the Good News. ■

Bob Vernon, a former Focus producer, in the film studio in Pomona, at far left.

At left, film editors work on one of the *Adventures in Odyssey* video projects for young children.

Opposite: The filming of *A Man Called Norman* with Mike Adkins, circa 1987.

A FATAL ADDICTION

WHEN SERIAL KILLER TED BUNDY was about to be executed, he requested a face-to-face interview with Dr. Dobson. During his years of incarceration, Bundy had come to recognize the tragic effects of pornography in his life, and he wanted to discuss with Dr. Dobson the factors that had contributed to his horrendous legacy of mass murder.

"Although he took full responsibility for his heinous crimes," Dr. Dobson recalls, "he also described how his first exposure to pornography during his teen years started him down a dark, dangerous, and evil road. The morning after Ted Bundy spoke with me—January 24, 1989—he was led to the electric chair, the confessed murderer of twenty-eight women."

Bundy's case dominated the news for weeks. Between seven hundred and eight hundred calls came in to the ministry within a single week, all seeking information about the meeting. Focus had the only tape available of the interview, and a media feeding frenzy set in. "Who are you guys?" the media would ask. "What can we give you to let us use that tape?" One network even offered half a million dollars for exclusive use of the tape for eighteen hours.

Dr. Dobson chose not to capitalize on this situation, but to honor Bundy's wishes. Instead of selling the interview tape in a bidding war, Focus gave it free to all sources and later used the interview to create a powerful video titled *Fatal Addiction*. All profits received from the video were used to fund additional efforts to combat pornography, an effort that continues to this day. ∎

All profits from *Fatal Addiction*, created from Dr. Dobson's interview with confessed killer Ted Bundy, have gone to help fund the fight against pornography— more than $700,000 to date.

Bundy met with Dr. Dobson, opposite, the night before his execution to explain how pornography impacted the course of his life.

THAT THE WORLD MAY KNOW

The staff and crew film set five of *That the World May Know* at the library in Ephesus, top, in 1999.

At right, a few of our *That the World May Know* resources created for families, small groups, schools, and churches.

Opposite: Ray Vander Laan, host of the video series, teaches a faith lesson at Herod, Israel.

IN 1993 JIM AND SHIRLEY DOBSON, through the encouragement and generosity of their friends Ed and Elsa Prince, took a trip with twenty-four others to the Holy Land. Their teacher and guide for that excursion was Ray Vander Laan, a Bible instructor from Michigan who had hosted many similar tours.

"Our trip did not concentrate primarily on the typical tourist attractions," Dr. Dobson explains. "We spent most of our time at a series of archaeological sites near Jerusalem, walking some of the same ground that Jesus walked during His earthly ministry. It was there that the Scriptures came alive for me like never before. For weeks after we returned, I dreamed about the trip almost every night. Many of the familiar stories from the Bible took on a whole new meaning as a result of that visit."

At one point during the tour, Dr. Dobson mentioned to Ed Prince that it was a shame so few people would ever get an opportunity to experience what they were seeing and hearing in Israel. Then he said, "We should produce a video about it." Ed eagerly replied, "Let's do it!"

Not long after returning to the States, the Prince family contributed the funds to videotape an entire seminar in Israel. The result was a five-volume series titled *That the World May Know: Faith Lessons*. The first set was released in 1995, and we immediately received enthusiastic feedback from churches, small groups, and even home-schooling families. Other editions soon followed. In 1999, the fifth set, which was filmed primarily in Turkey and focused on the early Christian church, was completed.

In addition, from our existing footage, Focus on the Family Films produced two separate television specials for Christmas and Easter. *Herod the Great, Jesus the King: The True Christmas Story* and *The Promise Kept: The True Easter Story* have both been aired on network television and made available for families to view in their homes.

"My only regret is that Ed Prince did not live to see this project come to fruition," Dr. Dobson says. "He passed away about a year before the first video was released. His fervent support from the very beginning made the entire endeavor possible. I have no doubt that he's rejoicing in heaven over the lives that have been touched through these videos." ∎

World Wide Ministry

TWENTY-FIVE YEARS AGO, WHEN FOCUS was in its infancy, words like "Internet," "dot com," and "web site" were a long way from entering our cultural lexicon. No one had any idea how these terms—and the technology they represent—would change our lives.

In recent years, however, the World Wide Web has become the predominant information source and communication tool for millions of people around the globe. Focus has seized opportunities presented by emerging technology to spread the Gospel of Jesus Christ and reinforce biblical values. We've seen the powerful potential to reach even more families by providing information through a medium that allows instant access to the best marriage and parenting materials available. And since the Lord challenged us to "enlarge our territory" in keeping with the prayer of Jabez (1 Chronicles 4:10), we've placed even more emphasis upon ministering via the Internet.

An average of forty-five thousand people per day visit www.family.org, Focus on the Family's home page, and this figure is consistently rising. Thousands of the folks who log on to our site are already friends of the ministry, but many others discover us while searching online for family-related help or advice. Our presence on the Internet has given us an unprecedented opportunity to introduce many new individuals and families to Focus—and ultimately to Christ.

Those who contact us belong to a wide variety of demographic groups: married couples, children, single parents, educators, grandparents, pastors and their wives, physicians, teenagers, college students, and more. Further, the struggles that prompt people to seek our assistance are as varied as the people themselves—the death of a spouse, marital infidelity, eating disorders, rebellious teens, post-abortive grief, strong-willed children, and so on. For all of these problems, there are resources, counsel, and encouragement available on our site.

Here are some of the ways in which we're taking advantage of this dynamic medium: Many areas online meet the needs of children and teens through www.clubhousemagazine.com, www.whitsend.org, www.briomag.com, www.breakawaymag.com, and www.lifeontheedge.com. These links all feature engaging articles, Q & A columns, reader forums, activity suggestions, poems, and games, and combine to give kids of all ages a safe place to explore issues of faith, family, and relationships.

Just a few of the web sites created for various Focus on the Family ministry efforts.

College students can click on www.boundless.org to access information they need to keep their faith strong. Cutting-edge articles express a cogent defense for a Christian worldview. The Focus on the Family Institute also has a forum, www.focusinstitute.com, where interested web users can learn the benefits of this esteemed academic program.

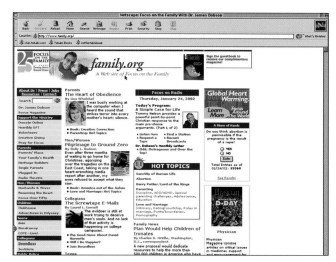

Families can find parenting and marriage topics addressed at www.family.org/parentsplace, www.family.org/married, www.pluggedinmag.com, and www.heritagebuilders.com. Also, single parents can get encouragement and practical advice from www.single-parentfamily.com.

Staying up to date on policy issues affecting the family is easy with www.citizenlink.org. This site enables people to take an active role in local, state, and federal issues. Parents needing help on the education front can find it at www.focusoneducation.com.

Pastors, too, can find support and direct assistance on www.parsonage.org, and the power of prayer is as strong as ever on www.ndptf.org and www.family.org/prayer.

Finally, those wanting information or help regarding pornography can find it on www.pureintimacy.org.

With the introduction of streaming media technology, bulletin boards, and live chat events, Focus on the Family will be able to provide more current information than ever before. Whether we are interacting with our friends and constituents personally or virtually, we will continue to faithfully provide support and encouragement to families everywhere. ∎

"I am thankful that your site was available at a time in which I had nowhere else to turn. Your articles provide openings for intimate, real communication between my husband and myself. We, by God's grace, are going to pick up the pieces and hope for the best relationship ever." —ANONYMOUS CONSTITUENT

FIGHTING FIRE WITH FIRE

No doubt about it: the availability of pornography on the Internet is a serious problem. Focus has tried to combat it—at least in a small way.

"While working in the Public Policy division as an Internet research analyst," says Steve Watters, "I was overwhelmed by all the bad news coming out about the spread of Internet pornography and the effect it was having on the families who were contacting the ministry. When Vice President Paul Hetrick mentioned one day that he was looking for anti-pornography projects to fund with revenue from the videotaped interview with Ted Bundy, I suggested we create the Pure Intimacy web site and promote it through a creative online advertising campaign."

In the summer of 1999, Focus started placing an ad that read, "Great Sex…Does Not Require a Modem." The ad appeared on the LookSmart search engine whenever a visitor would enter the words *sex*, *porn*, *pornography,* or *nude*.

"LookSmart told us that the response to the ad was more than twenty times higher than the average online advertisement usually receives," says Watters.

PART SIX

BEYOND THE BORDERS

A Message Brought to a Needy World

"GO INTO ALL THE WORLD AND PREACH THE GOOD NEWS TO ALL CREATION."

[MARK 16:15]

Many friends and supporters of Focus assume that our current international outreach is the fulfillment of some grand design. Not so! In fact, in the early days of this ministry, most of us were not thinking in terms of a "global vision." We were much too busy answering letters and calls, recording broadcasts, packaging books and tapes, and generally trying to keep up with each day's demands.

A few longtime staff members recall one of our first chapel services, where Dr. Ted Engstrom shared his belief that Focus would some day have a presence in countries around the world. Many people in chapel that day either chuckled, thinking the idea was too far-fetched to consider, or panicked, wondering what that might mean for their already daunting workload!

It wasn't too surprising when our neighbors in Canada wanted to create a stronger presence for Focus. After all, Canadian families were experiencing many of the same struggles. It also seemed like a natural step to begin translating broadcasts and resources into Spanish to reach more families in the United States.

Later, when individuals and groups in Europe and South Africa began requesting the use of our resources and programs, we were more than happy to help. We were soon amazed to find doors opening in Australia, Russia, and China. Our international ministry began expanding with such incredible results, so clearly orchestrated by God, that we were in awe!

Broadcasts, magazines, books, tapes, videos, and special events have all been utilized by Focus on the Family's associate offices around the world. The Internet is also opening new ministry avenues not limited by borders or time zones. And our global ministry is "hands-on" as well: For several years, the editors of our teen magazines, *Brio* and *Breakaway*, have led groups of young people into countries where they serve the needy and share God's love.

We began our international outreach without knowing exactly where God would lead, and we honestly don't know what doors He will open in the years ahead. But we are thrilled beyond words to participate in His ministry throughout the world!

Focus's International division staff poses with flags from their native countries. Clocks on the wall in the back show the time in other parts of the world.

OPEN DOORS

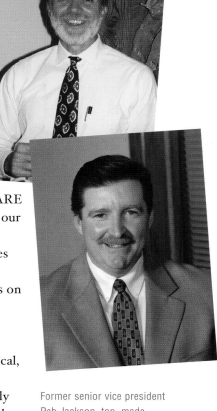

FROM THE VERY BEGINNING, Focus has received requests for help from all over the world. Dr. Dobson's early books and the *Focus on the Family* film series soon found their way into many other countries, and there was clear demand for the radio broadcast to be aired internationally. In fact, our ministry's venture into Canada in 1983 was so overwhelmingly positive that it provided the encouragement and motivation to continue reaching out to other nations.

As a result, we formed a close relationship in the mid-1980s with our friends from CARE Trust in the United Kingdom. Lyndon Bowring, Charlie Colchester, and Rob Parsons became our true "comrades in arms," an alliance that led to the establishment of Care for the Family.

It quickly became apparent that the message of strong family ties and biblical values held universal appeal—from Russia to South Africa, China to Japan, Norway to the South Pacific. Subsequently, staff members made many visits following the establishment of Focus on the Family in Canada and the United Kingdom to Europe, South Africa, and Moscow. Everywhere we have been invited, our help was met with openness and enthusiasm.

Jim Daly, vice president of Marketing and International, observes, "Too often, the impressions we get from our media about people from other countries are only related to political, cultural, religious, or economic differences," he says. "But the concept of 'family' resonates strongly with all people, regardless of other differences. Whether it's an impoverished family in a small South African village or an affluent couple in one of America's large cities, we find the same basic family concerns: premarital sex, marital strife and divorce, parenting dilemmas, and communication breakdowns between family members."

Governments, too, see the vital link of family as being essential to a strong national infrastructure. For example, a growing number of foreign governments are taking our sexual abstinence programs and implementing them in their schools as a response to the epidemic of HIV/AIDS. And when the Italian government was debating whether to recognize homosexual marriages, it was Focus that provided materials that were read on its Senate floor.

"Because Focus on the Family provides real solutions—ones that not only save lives but strengthen individuals and families—there is overwhelming receptivity to our resources," Jim says. "As a result, many people are coming to the Lord through the common language of the family." ∎

Former senior vice president Peb Jackson, top, made many of our early ministry contacts in other countries.

Jim Daly, above, is currently the vice president of Marketing and International for Focus on the Family.

Opposite: Translator on staff for Family Focus Japan, Tsuneo Maejima, and his wife, Harumi, and daughters (left to right), Koloko, Kanade, and Tae.

"Dr. Dobson started Focus on the Family in the 1970s when easy divorce laws and liberalization of family policy were only just getting going in countries like Australia and New Zealand. Back then Dr. Dobson could see the problems and where the family was going. Today we have inherited the destruction of the nuclear family in all of our countries. But we stand in the gap—and it's a very exciting place to be."

— CRAIG HEILMANN, INTERNATIONAL DIRECTOR, FOCUS ON THE FAMILY NEW ZEALAND

Global Outreach

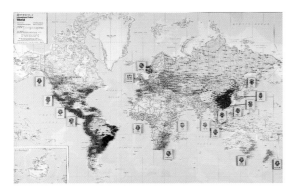

One of the maps featured on our tour shows the international reach of the *Focus* broadcast.

Opposite: Dr. Darrel Reid, president of Focus on the Family Canada, with Dr. Dobson.

One of the rare instances when Dr. Dobson felt an unmistakable calling from God to move Focus in a new direction occurred during a broadcast taping in March 2001. Dr. Bruce Wilkinson had been invited to discuss his book *The Prayer of Jabez*, which focuses on 1 Chronicles 4:10: "Oh, that you would bless me and enlarge my territory! Let your hand be with me, and keep me from harm so that I will be free from pain." Over the course of the conversation, Dr. Wilkinson challenged Focus on the Family to extend its reach to every country.

"What took place next was unexpected and deeply moving," Dr. Dobson recalls. "The Spirit of the Lord seemed to descend on our studio, touching [co-host] Gary Bender and me, the technicians, and all the observers in the gallery. Each of us was aware that something very unusual was happening. Clearly, we were being urged—not by Bruce Wilkinson, but by God— to expand our vision and broaden our horizons as never before."

Not coincidentally, members of both the U.S. and Canadian boards of directors, along with Focus on the Family Canada President Dr. Darrel Reid, arrived in Colorado Springs that afternoon for our winter meetings, and they also caught the spirit of the moment.

"As we discussed the following day what had happened in the studio," Dr. Dobson continues, "we again felt the leading of the Lord to expand our outreach, not just internationally, but also to families in the United States whose lives we have not yet impacted in a significant way."

As a result, Focus's board of directors encouraged the development of new initiatives to four targeted groups, including young families just beginning the adventures of marriage and parenthood; minority families from diverse ethnic backgrounds; individuals and families who become acquainted with Focus through the Internet; and families residing in countries not yet reached by the ministry. Those four initiatives provide the driving force behind much of our effort today. ■

"God has blessed Focus on the Family with remarkable growth. As we move forward with goals to reach many new young families of every nationality—both in the U.S. and in every nation of the world—we continue to pray for Dr. and Mrs. Dobson and all who make the ministry possible. They have been remarkably gifted by God, and we thank them for their faithfulness and willingness to bless and touch so many lives."

—Elsa D. Prince Broekhuizen, chairman of E.O.P. Management Company LLC and Focus on the Family board member

Focus Around the World

From day one our leaders have prayed, "Lord, we will serve You wherever You lead us. Just show us the way." We've been delighted—and pleasantly surprised —at how God has opened doors for our ministry throughout the world. No one knew twenty-five years ago just how far-reaching our products and resources might be. To date, we have almost twenty international associate offices:

Focus on the Family Canada—established in 1983. With offices in Langley, British Columbia, our ally across our northern border distributes magazines and carries radio broadcasts on over 125 facilities. Focus Canada is actively involved in public policy issues, sponsors the Ottawa Conference on the Family, and receives medical advice from the Canadian Physicians' Resource Council.

Care for the Family (United Kingdom)— established in 1988. Our ministry partner in the United Kingdom has presented a series of family-life seminars throughout the British Isles, with attendees numbering more than twenty thousand. The Care for the Family staff produces resources on marriage and parenting, along with its own magazine.

Focus on the Family Southern Africa (Botswana, Lesotho, Malawi, Mozambique, Namibia, South Africa, Zambia, and Zimbabwe)—established in 1992. Headquartered in Kwa Zulu Natal, South Africa, this associate has placed broadcasts on nearly forty stations in the region. In addition, the organization is ministering to pastors and their families and developing an abstinence outreach to teenagers.

Focus on the Family Australia—established in 1993. The rapidly growing Australian office has placed radio programs on more than 130 outlets and has established an effective counseling ministry. In addition, the *How to Drug-Proof Your Kids* program and curriculum equips parents to talk with their children about saying no to drugs. This program has served as a model for other international associate offices.

Dr. Darrel Reid and Focus on the Family Canada board members, top, at the site of their new offices in Langley, British Columbia.

Above, the Focus on the Family Canada staff in the Vancouver, British Columbia, office.

At left, a Life on the Edge Tour event in Toronto, Canada.

Japan's *Family Focus* magazine.

Sam Kang, voice of the *Focus on the Family* broadcast in Korea.

Family Focus Japan—established in 1995. This office has widely distributed Japanese versions of Focus video products, including Dr. Dobson's original film series; *Sex, Lies and...the Truth*; *Life on the Edge*; and *That the World May Know*. A translated version of Dr. Dobson's ninety-second radio commentary also airs in some highly populated regions.

Focus on the Chinese Family, North America—established in 1996, and Taiwan—established in 1998. With offices in Southern California and Taiwan, this associate produces Chinese translations of Focus on the Family books and publishes a monthly magazine that includes articles from the U.S. version and Dr. Dobson's "Solid Answers" column. China National Radio airs the Mandarin translation of Dr. Dobson's ninety-second commentary from Beijing on more than four hundred stations.

Fokus Pada Keluarga (Indonesia)—established in 1996. This effort began by airing the Indonesian version of the ninety-second commentary, and families across the thirteen thousand islands that make up the country now hear the program. The office produces a monthly magazine and has arranged for the translation and distribution of many Focus resources.

Focus on the Family Philippines—established in 1996. This office broadcasts the *Focus* radio program, distributes resources to bookstores across the country, and has launched an abstinence campaign.

Focus on the Family Korea—established in 1996. Nearly six hundred of Dr. Dobson's radio programs have been translated and produced in Korean. Focus on the Family Korea has also held seminars to strengthen Christian marriages and families.

Enfoque a la Familia (Costa Rica)—established in 1998. Through the leadership of this Central American office, the fifteen-minute Spanish radio program now airs on nearly twelve hundred stations in thirty-two countries. Eleven of the eighteen Latin American countries have established *El Sexo, Las Mentiras y La Verdad* (adapted from our *Sex, Lies, and...the Truth* program) as their official sex education curriculum.

Focus on the Family Nigeria—established in 1998. The Nigerian office has been instrumental in showing the *Sex, Lies and...the Truth* video in schools and in distributing Christian materials for families. Thousands of students have responded to the abstinence message.

Focus on the Family Netherlands—established in 1998. The Netherlands associate office provides resources to Dutch families who face the same stresses and breakdown as families the world over. Life on the Edge conferences have been held with hundreds of teens and parents attending. Heritage Builders events have also had great response.

Focus on the Family New Zealand–established in 1998. After the *Focus on the Family* radio program had aired over the national broadcast network for some time, a Focus associate office was established to meet the listeners' needs and to address a broad spectrum of issues across the country.

Focus on the Family Malaysia—established in 1998. Dr. Dobson's ninety-second radio commentary airs on a national network and is played in more than two hundred Kentucky Fried Chicken restaurants and 280 supermarkets nationwide. His family advice column appears in Malaysia's leading English newspaper. The staff is developing family-life seminars and workplace programs for corporations.

Focus on the Family Singapore—established in 1999. This office has facilitated family workshops and initiated a phone counseling service. Many of the callers respond as a result of hearing Dr. Dobson's ninety-second radio commentary, which airs five times each day.

Focus on the Family East Africa—established in 2000. Headquartered in Nairobi, Kenya, this associate serves a region of about 100 million people in Tanzania, Uganda, and Kenya. Staff members distribute Christian materials and offer marriage seminars and premarital counseling. They have also had success with Life on the Edge conferences, and events for fathers.

Focus on the Family Egypt—established in 2001. Representing our first associate office in the Middle East, Focus on the Family Egypt has started translating *Adventures in Odyssey* videos into Arabic to reach children. They are also working to develop pro-life resources.

Focus on the Family Belgium—established in 2002. This office provides a range of resources and services to strengthen families adversely affected by a culture in severe moral decline. The associate is focusing on distributing Heritage Builders curriculum for families and churches and other materials for youth. ∎

MANY LANGUAGES, ONE MESSAGE OF HOPE

It's estimated that a few thousand people heard the first *Focus on the Family* broadcast when it aired in select U.S. regions. Twenty-five years later, millions of people around the world are being reached by a Focus-produced broadcast each day. Our broadcasts are now heard in fifteen languages in more than 107 countries worldwide, including Chinese, English, French, Indonesian, Italian, Japanese, Korean, Norwegian, Polish, Portuguese, Russian, Slovak, and Spanish.

Enfoque a la Familia, the Spanish-language version, is heard on more than fifteen hundred radio facilities in thirty-four countries. Dr. Dobson's translated ninety-second commentary is heard on state-owned stations across China. Dr. Dobson is known as "Dr. Du" in China.

Darrell Eash, manager of Spanish broadcasting (left), with Roberto Cruz, the "Spanish Dr. Dobson," heard on the *Enfoque a la Familia* broadcast.

Some of the logos designed for ministry efforts in various languages throughout the world (left to right): French, Portuguese, Japanese, Chinese, Indonesian, Korean, Spanish, and Russian.

INTERNATIONAL PRIDE

First prize in the Focus on the Family Malaysia photo competition.

Malaysia staff hold a family event to make people aware of their ministry.

The grand prize winner in the Focus on the Family Malaysia family photo competition.

Focus on the Chinese Family produces and distributes resources in North America as well as China.

Children's smiles translate the same in any language!

Jimmy Oentoro, president of Focus on the Family Indonesia, welcomes H. B. London to the Light the Nation pastors' gathering.

More than two thousand pastors came forward for prayer following the two-hour message in Jakarta.

"*Just as all English-speaking countries around the world are culturally different, so the Asian countries represent individually unique challenges to answer the problems besetting their family structures, some of which are steeped in traditions over a thousand years old. Fortunately, the growing global youth culture is providing some commonality upon which solutions may be offered. Beyond this phenomenon, however, Asian families must be reached within prevailing worldviews of Buddhism or Islam.*"

—KEN LANE, DIRECTOR OF INTERNATIONAL RELATIONS FOR EURASIA

International directors pose with Dr. Dobson and Focus leaders outside the Focus executive wing during the 1997 Directors' Conference.

Focus staff member Reed Olson with the First Lady of Guatemala, Patricia Escobar de Arzu, who invited a U.S. team to hold evangelical workshops for the Guatemalan police force.

Guatemalan officers reading their new Bibles. Many have come to Christ through this effort.

Focus partnered with First Lady Patricia Escobar de Arzu, Randy Green, and two international Bible ministries to provide fifty thousand Bibles for Guatemala's schools, military, and police officers.

Students in Campo Grande, Brazil (near Rio), show their pledge cards after hearing the No Apologies message. Over five thousand decisions for abstinence were made.

South African families face many challenges in their culture today, and Focus offers hope and help through programs and resources.

Shirley Dobson greets children in a Masai tribal village near Nairobi, Kenya, during a 1988 missionary trip.

"The United Kingdom has a population that is about one-fifth the size of the United States. For every Christian in the United Kingdom, there are forty in the United States. We have many needs in our country but the demolition of marriage in our nation makes most of the other social policy issues that we tackle a sideshow. The state of marriage in our country is in crisis, and as director of Care for the Family, I feel we must do something about these marriages. It is an enormous challenge, but we are encouraged—

CARE FOR THE FAMILY

IN 1987, JIM AND SHIRLEY DOBSON TRAVELED to England to work on a writing project. While there, Dr. Dobson received a phone call from a stranger—Lyndon Bowring, who said he was with an organization called CARE Trust.

"He asked if he and his wife, Celia, could take Shirley and me to a special parade where all the regalia and the beauty of the British monarchy would be on display," Dr. Dobson recalls. "We agreed and got acquainted with them. They became friends that I will cherish for the rest of my life."

Dr. Dobson and Lyndon Bowring had many conversations about the needs of families in the United Kingdom. It was later decided that CARE Trust should start a division called Care for the Family, which Focus would help fund. That was in 1988, and a board member of CARE Trust named Rob Parsons was asked to lead the organization. As a busy lawyer, husband, and father of two young children, he knew firsthand the pressures on young families—and he sensed God leading him to leave his law practice for this new ministry.

Beginning with three employees, Care for the Family has grown to more than sixty staff members. The organization has a mailing list of over 100,000 and ministers to people across the United Kingdom through resources, media, seminars, and special events. This has been achieved in a country where Christian radio is scarce and only one in ten people attend church.

Rob recalls the story of a police officer who reprimanded a man for assaulting his wife's lover—and then gave the man a copy of Rob's book *Loving Against the Odds*. The man later wrote Care for the Family saying, "Thank you for saving my marriage. If it weren't for your kindness, I would have given up. I have forgiven my wife for her affair. I realize now why it happened."

Another woman described her marriage in a letter to the ministry, saying, "Divorce was not far away. The situation seemed hopeless. My marriage of sixteen years was crumbling around me, and it seemed that there was nothing I could do about it. It was at that moment that my husband and I decided to watch a video featuring Rob Parsons. He began with the words 'I don't know you,' yet it seemed that he was talking directly to us. Every situation he described had happened in our marriage. Afterward, we talked—really talked—for the first time in years."

In recent years, new doors of outreach have opened in the secular community as Care for the Family has participated in events such as National Parenting Week. The ministry also offers a seminar called "The Heart of a Parent," which is designed for diverse audiences across the United Kingdom.

"Our aim is simple and straightforward—to strengthen the family and help the hurting," Rob says. "We are privileged to see God use Care for the Family to accomplish those goals in amazing ways." ■

Single-Parent and Clergy Appreciation Week events sponsored by Care for the Family, shown at top and middle.

Above, Sir Cliff Richard joins Jonathan Booth and Rob Parsons on the Care for the Family Bike Ride.

Jonathan Booth and Rob Parsons, opposite, lead Care for the Family in the United Kingdom.

Focus on the Family
Southern Africa

Jim and Shirley Dobson visited South Africa with several board members and friends in 1997.

Opposite: Zulu children in South Africa show off their *No Apologies* workbooks, part of the abstinence curriculum created by Focus and translated for use around the world.

FOCUS ON THE FAMILY SOUTHERN AFRICA, one of our oldest associate offices, was started in 1992 by Danie van den Heever, a Harvard Business School graduate who volunteered his time. Van den Heever was able to get the *Focus on the Family* broadcast on to radio stations, and it now reaches an estimated two million listeners.

In 1997, Dr. Dobson visited the offices of Focus on the Family Southern Africa, giving the ministry a much-needed boost. Until that time, he had been somewhat skeptical that his message could be relevant to people of such far-flung regions and cultures.

South Africa had a unique challenge to overcome when apartheid came to an end. In 1994, it was on the knife-edge of entering into a bloodbath or receiving a miracle. It got a miracle: When Nelson Mandela became president, a peaceful transition of power occurred. Immediately, the new leader instituted efforts not at revenge, but racial reconciliation.

"We still have the legacy of apartheid and it will take a while to fully integrate the races, but the family message is universal," van den Heever states. "It is providential that Focus on the Family opened its offices right in the middle of this dramatic shift in direction."

Focus on the Family Southern Africa works primarily through churches, and most Focus resources and broadcasts are in English. Broadcasts have recently been added in Zulu and Afrikaans.

"The Lord brings us talented, well-placed people," van den Heever says. "They can play a vital role in changing the culture of Africa. The abstinence message of the *No Apologies* film and curriculum is also being a tremendous catalyst in reaching our young people with a message of hope that they have a future worth living for." ∎

"We at Focus on the Family Southern Africa are faced with just about every issue you would like to think about. The biggest is HIV/AIDS. We believe that Focus right now is strategically placed to make a difference within our country and the countries north of us. The job is enormous—but we have hope. And we've had government ministers come to Focus to ask for help, so the Lord is at work. He is empowering us and raising up people to do a fantastic job; so just watch."

—MALCOLM ST. CLAIR, FOCUS ON THE FAMILY SOUTHERN AFRICA

Focus on the Chinese Family

BIBLICAL TRUTHS RESONATE IN THE HEARTS of people whether or not they are followers of Jesus Christ. This principle holds true for men and women around the world, regardless of color, economic status, or political orientation.

In 1997 the program director for China National Radio in Beijing was awakened at three o'clock in the morning by the enthusiastic president of a Chinese-language radio station in Los Angeles. The urgent call was to announce his discovery of a family-based radio program in Mandarin called *Focus on the Family Commentary*. Once the Beijing official reviewed the program, he said, "This is the best educational information on the family that I have ever heard."

The *Mandarin Commentary* is produced by Focus on the Chinese Family (FOCF) in Los Angeles, and it has been broadcast across a rapidly changing China since 1997. The estimated daily listening audience is more than 200 million people nationwide. As a direct result of the commentary's broad acceptance and deep impact, remarkable doors continue to open for Focus's outreach into mainland China—most notably, a series of family consultations hosted by the All China Women's Federation and the China Social Workers Association. These gatherings began when officials approached Focus on the Family for help with revisions being made to China's Family Law policy.

The desire to better understand Focus's mission resulted in a visit by six delegates from Beijing, who traveled to Colorado Springs in November 2000. The leader of the delegation, Zhang Xiao Qing, revealed during discussions that she was one of the pioneers for adoption in China. A couple that works at Focus, Scott and Cindy Covington, had recently adopted their daughter from China, and we introduced Zhang Xiao Qing to Cindy, a Chinese-American, over lunch.

As their conversation unfolded, they discovered that it was probably Xiao Qing who had approved the Covingtons' adoption of Stephanie. The lunch also provided an opportunity to clear up some long-held misconceptions, as Xiao Qing and the other delegates realized that

American families did not mistreat their adopted Chinese children, as had been reported in mainland China.

While Focus on the Chinese Family has been a strategic partner in working with mainland China, meeting the needs of Chinese families in North America remains its primary objective. This has been a daunting task since the inception of FOCF, due largely to the diversity and fragmentation within the Chinese community. The constituency is a cross-cultural mosaic—multilingual, multiethnic, and multigenerational.

While individuals identify themselves as American-born, Canadian-born, or overseas-born, families also define themselves as being from mainland China, Hong Kong, or Taiwan. Identity crises abound as some family members fiercely fight to preserve their

Stephanie Covington, above, was adopted from China by Focus employees Scott and Cindy Covington.

Chinese traditions while others seek to assimilate into American or Canadian culture. In addition to the cultural struggles, of course, are the typical everyday challenges that all families face. This is the community that the FOCF team feels passionately called to serve, offering hope and help for Chinese families of every variety. ∎

THE MESSAGE IS GETTING THROUGH

Increasingly alarmed at the rate its families are falling apart, Chinese officials have been seeking solutions—and turning to Focus for help. In March 2000, the All China Women's Federation and China Social Workers Association asked us to provide input during a rare revision of China's Family Law policy. In May, they invited Focus representatives to meet with Chinese delegates and discuss practical ways to address issues impacting China's families.

The meetings were such a success that six delegates representing the two organizations spent two days at the Focus campus in November 2000 to understand more fully our ministry and mission. Zhang Xiao Qing, president of the Social Workers Association, led the delegation. Second in command was Chen Xin Xin, a social researcher for the Women's Federation and marriage and family specialist in the media. Both women have a passion to help hurting families and dream of seeing an organization like Focus on the Family in China some day. The delegates were profoundly impacted by our Christian perspective—and by meeting Dr. Dobson, for whom they have great respect after reading his books and listening to his radio broadcast in China.

Opposite: Meeting with social workers at the All China Women's Federation in Beijing, China. Speaking is Dr. Wei-Jen Huang, professor of psychology at Northwestern University and a good friend of Focus on the Family.

A MESSAGE OF PURITY

Sex, Lies and...the Truth curriculum under guard in the presidential palace in Guatemala City.

IN MAY 1992, FOCUS RECEIVED A LETTER from Humberto Belli, the minister of education of Nicaragua, requesting biblical sex education materials for use in his public school system. For years, the Marxist government had caused much suffering among the Nicaraguan people, but a new democratic government was trying to restore their faith and dignity.

Unfortunately, we didn't have much to send Mr. Belli at the time, though our abstinence video for teens, *Sex, Lies and...the Truth* (*SLT*), was soon to be released in English. But two years later, after *SLT* was translated into Spanish, Focus fulfilled the Nicaraguan government's request to provide it to 2,768 schools. The program was well received.

In subsequent months, we concluded that other Latin American governments and educators would have a similar interest in *SLT* and began promoting it throughout Central and South America and the Caribbean. Within months, reports began pouring in that many who had taken the course were also making decisions to accept Christ—a surprising development given that *SLT* presented a moral viewpoint but was not overtly Christian.

Reed Olson, Focus's director of international relations to Latin America and the Caribbean, explains: "I failed to understand what God was doing with this resource until I traveled to Santiago, Chile, in November 1996 to participate in an *SLT* seminar for three hundred government, church, and school leaders. As I sat in a large auditorium, the Lord unexpectedly impressed a clear image on my mind. I saw a map of Central and South America, and it was covered with long, brown grass. I was walking on the map, heading from south to north. I held a matchbox in my hand, and as I walked, I removed matches from the box, lit them, and dropped them to the ground. A small fire started wherever I dropped a flaming match, a fire that spread and grew out from the center. I watched as several fires started this way until the Lord spoke to my heart with His unmistakable voice. 'The matches are *SLT*,' He said, 'and I've anointed this material to bring many people to Myself.' I sat there stunned, having never experienced anything like that in my twenty-plus years of knowing the Lord."

In the months that followed, Reed and his staff began sharing *SLT* with Latin American governments and looking for open doors to bring the abstinence message into public schools. Requests came from the president of Costa Rica, the vice president of Ecuador, and

Vice President of International Jim Daly, left, with the first lady of Costa Rica and Sixto Porras, director of Enfoque a la Familia, Costa Rica.

Opposite: Teens in Panama make pledges for sexual purity in response to an *SLT* presentation by Sixto Porras.

the first ladies of Guatemala, Panama, Peru, and El Salvador. The education ministers of Paraguay, Colombia, and Honduras were also eager to use the video. We supplied materials for thousands of schools and partnered with other in-country organizations to distribute and teach the course in school classrooms throughout the region.

At first, dozens of kids came to Christ as they embraced our message of sexual purity, repented of their sins, and put their faith in Jesus. Over and over again, entire classrooms were touched by the message of forgiveness and second chances, leaving students and their teachers weeping and hungry for God. To date, over 450,000 sexual purity pledges have been reported from fifteen Latin American countries alone. Every month, many more respond.

But the story doesn't end there. In 1998 we launched our newest abstinence product: *No Apologies: The Truth About Life, Love, and Sex*. It, too, caught the attention of the world. What God started in Latin America, He soon expanded to Eastern and Western Europe, Asia, and Africa—forty-nine nations in all. Scores of young people have begun living lives of character in places where AIDS and sexual immorality are ravaging their lands. Felipe, a sixteen-year-old from Brazil, heard the three-day presentation and said, "I would like to see other young people with the same vision, and I will do whatever I can to present it to them. I know we can remain abstinent until we marry if we want to."

Clarissa, a nineteen-year-old college student from Rio de Janeiro, said, "I am a Christian, but I'd never learned the importance of staying abstinent in such a clear way. I want to remain abstinent until marriage and teach these concepts to my children and to as many people as possible." Just two weeks after hearing the message of *No Apologies*, she spoke to over fifteen hundred students about her commitment to sexual purity.

Thousands of teenagers and young adults are choosing abstinence. Hundreds of teachers are volunteering their time to present the program to students and mentoring teens by leading lives of character. Truly, what God spoke to Habakkuk thousands of years ago is occurring all over the world: "Look at the nations and watch—and be utterly amazed. For I am going to do something in your days that you would not believe, even if you were told" (Habakkuk 1:5). We are indeed utterly amazed at what God is doing through our ministry. ■

South African students, top, show their pledge cards after going through the *No Apologies* program in their school.

Above, students in Thailand view the *SLT* video as part of their abstinence curriculum.

Opposite: Teens affirm their pledges to abstain from sex until marriage during a "Purity Day" celebration on February 14, 2002, in Bangkok, Thailand, where Focus's abstinence curriculum has been endorsed by the government.

"It has been a privilege to share with adolescents such an important message. It was wonderful to see understanding cross their faces, to actually see how the truth hit home. The kids actually saw themselves in the different situations presented—but above all, they saw that it is possible to start over again, totally free!"

—THEA MATHERS, KWA ZULU NATAL, *No Apologies* TEACHER

THE FIRST NINE MONTHS

Bruce Peppin, above, in his office in the late 1980s, when *The First Nine Months* was created.

Below, several foreign translations of the booklet that is still being used to help save babies throughout the world.

A cover image from one of the booklets, opposite, shows the development of a pre-born child in the fifth month.

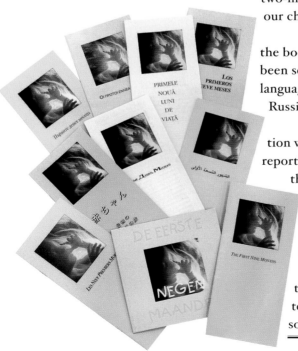

OVER THE YEARS, WE'VE SEEN GOD use many of our efforts in ways we couldn't have imagined. One small resource that has had a big impact in the United States and around the world is a booklet created years ago.

Longtime Focus staff member Bruce Peppin recalls how this came about: "One of the most significant projects I ever worked on was a little pro-life booklet. When the abortion debate was raging in the 1980s, Focus wanted to provide materials to help the three thousand or so Crisis Pregnancy Centers that were counseling women and saving many babies. I was given the assignment to determine what we should do to assist them."

Bruce sought input from CPC leaders, several of whom requested a resource that clearly presented a baby's development prior to birth without any reference to abortion. The idea was to let the facts speak for themselves.

"We tracked down photos of babies in utero and the latest medical information to create a new booklet, which we titled *The First Nine Months*," Bruce recalls. "It became the first four-color booklet produced by the ministry, and the photos depicting life before birth really did make a strong argument against abortion."

The response was dramatic. Within the first year of publication, thousands of copies were requested, and numerous stories came back about mothers who decided to give their babies life after reading the booklet. One pastor wrote us to say that he gave *The First Nine Months* to a woman seeking counsel concerning her unwed daughter's pregnancy. The daughter, who was considering abortion, read it and decided to deliver and keep her child. He said, "I hadn't seen this woman in church for months and it warmed my heart to see a delicate little two-month-old in her arms. What a happy grandmother she was! Dr. Dobson, that child was in our church because of your ministry."

Despite the robust response in the United States, we were surprised at how widely the booklet became disseminated overseas. To date, more than two million copies have been sent out both in this country and abroad. The booklet has been published in eleven languages, including Arabic, Bulgarian, Croatian, French, Greek, Hindi, Japanese, Romanian, Russian, Spanish, and Ukranian.

Between 1999 and 2000, more than twenty thousand copies of the Bulgarian translation were distributed in over ten cities to women's clinics and pro-life outreaches. Television reports at the end of 2000 stated that for the first time in several years, the birth rate outpaced the abortion rate in Bulgaria. Our distributor, Cheri Fresonke of Truth Ministries, stated, "I was overjoyed to hear that. I asked myself what factors were involved that helped to lower Bulgaria's abortion rate. I know the brochures were a major factor in this. Thanks to Focus for being a major factor in Bulgaria for this important work. *Slava na Boga*— Glory to God!"

Bruce sums up the impact of this booklet: "There is no question in my mind that hundreds, perhaps thousands, of people are alive today because their mothers chose to give them life after reading *The First Nine Months*. It just goes to show that God can do something great with our humblest offerings." ∎

The Heart to Serve

Nothing exemplifies our heart for international ministry more than the annual missions trips sponsored by *Brio*, our magazine for teen girls. *Brio*'s staff began offering cross-cultural outreaches in 1996 with a trip to Bolivia. That trip was so successful that in 1998, two hundred girls went on a two-week missions trip to Costa Rica. In 1999, nearly four hundred served in Rio de Janeiro, Brazil, and the following year, 460 participants returned to Brazil. In 2001, more than four hundred teens traveled to Caracas, Venezuela, where nearly three thousand people came to know the Lord through evangelistic drama presentations.

Teen missions trips include both work, above, and worship.

Opposite: Teen girls enjoy an evening "FUAGNEM" service — that's "Fired up and Going Nuts Every Minute"— on the *Brio* to Rio trip in 2000.

Approximately fifteen hundred girls apply each year, but the trips can accommodate no more than five hundred. All the participants meet in Miami, Florida, for three days of intensive drama training before heading to South America. There, the girls are kept busy performing street drama, painting orphanages, cleaning local churches, playing with orphaned children, and so on. Each evening, the entire group shares in a praise and worship rally, led by Christian music artists. Then *Brio* editor Susie Shellenberger gives the teens a challenging message.

"Our hope is that many of these girls will feel the call to missions or at least develop a heart for serving those less fortunate," Susie says. "We also want teens to realize how fortunate they are compared to millions around the world. It's our prayer that God will work in the lives of these girls to produce eternal changes and even call some of them into full-time ministry."

Seventeen-year-old Angelina Mier of Boulder, Colorado, went on the trip to Venezuela in 2001. She recalls, "One day after our drama presentation, our translator told the crowd to come and talk with him if they wanted to accept Jesus into their hearts. Soon, a huge line of people were waiting to talk to the translator. Tears were streaming down their faces. It was so amazing to see the power of God and His Word! Almost three thousand people came to know the Lord during that trip, and it was such a blessing to be a part of God's work. It is so cool to think that all those people will be with me when I get to heaven."

Michelle Dawson also participated in the Venezuela trip, and she recalls an incident that impacted her spiritual life. "One day, I had just finished praying with four ladies and told them we had some Spanish Bibles for them. I went to get them and found to my dismay that there were only two left. I brought what we had to the women, and all four of them reached out eagerly, as if they were starving and the Bibles were food. The ladies who didn't get one had such looks of disappointment on their faces. Right then, I found a new appreciation for the power of the Word of God. How often do we take for granted this precious gift God has given us? Way too often." ∎

TEENS ON A MISSION

Breakaway *guys brave the heat on the 2001 trip to Venezuela.*

Teens help clean up after mudslides near Caracas in 2001.

Breakaway *guys in Caracas, Venezuela, 2001.*

One girl bows in prayer after the drama team's presentation.

Both *Brio* and *Breakaway* readers have participated in recent trips, which were characterized by both physical labor and a deeper awareness of God's work.

Brio *girls share team devotions every morning.*

Drama participants witness to local children after performances.

Brio *editor Susie Shellenberger speaks to teens in Rio de Janeiro in 2000.*

A Brio girl shares with a local child during the Rio missions trip.

Brio *girls plant trees at one of the schools in Caracas, Venezuela, 2001.*

"My sixteen-year-old daughter, Rachel, heard about the missions trip 'Brio to Rio' when she was fourteen, and asked if she could participate. It was a step of faith for her because she didn't know anyone else going. It was a step of faith for us because she is a juvenile diabetic on an insulin pump, and she would have to manage on her own in a foreign country. The trip was great, and she especially enjoyed meeting so many committed teenage Christians, something that is scarce in her small, rural school. It gave her a sense of identity and confidence in her Christian walk, and she has not been afraid to stand alone and be different in the midst of peer pressure. It was a major milestone in her life at a key time. Thanks, Brio!" —ELLEN WILLOUGHBY, CONSTITUENT

MAKING A DIFFERENCE

ONE REASON OUR INTERNATIONAL OUTREACH has been so effective is that God continually brings people to partner with us at just the right time.

For instance, a few years ago we heard that the relief organization Samaritan's Purse was helping refugees in Kosovo, and we thought it presented a great opportunity to distribute an Albanian version of Dr. Dobson's book *When God Doesn't Make Sense*. The challenge was to find someone who could translate a large manuscript within a tight time frame.

After a few false starts, we stumbled across a wonderful woman named Besa. She had come to visit Focus and talk with the *Clubhouse* magazine staff because she worked on a children's publication in Tirana. She was introduced to our International department staff members, who immediately asked if she could help with the translation. Without hesitation, Besa agreed to the project, and the book was completed in early January 2000. Since then, thousands of copies have been distributed.

On another occasion, staff member Susie Sanguinetti received a phone call from a contact in Eastern Europe. He wanted to know if Focus had a radio broadcast translated in Slovak. Unfortunately, we didn't, and there was no budget to develop one.

"A half hour later," Susie recalls, "one of the guys from the Public Affairs department came into my office and said he had just returned from an event with some donors. One of them had a heart for Slovakia, and her foundation would help fund any resources we could develop. Hence the birth of Dr. Dobson's ninety-second commentary in Slovak, which has now been airing for several years."

Susie tells of how another God-ordained partnership was formed. A man from the Ukraine visited Focus and told her about a crisis pregnancy center that was being started in a hospital where abortions were performed. He wanted to know if Focus could provide materials to be used in that effort. We had only the booklet *The First Nine Months* in Russian and nothing in Ukrainian. The Russian booklet would work, but it was not ideal.

"Soon after the man left, I received a phone call about a donor who was of Ukrainian origin and wanted to support any Ukrainian translations we would like to do," Susie says. "The following year we had four booklets—including *The First Nine Months* and *Post-Abortion Syndrome*—translated for the Ukraine. These have been widely distributed and used very effectively."

Susie speaks for all of her colleagues in the International department when she says, "God has a marvelous way of linking us with people at precisely the right moment to accomplish His purposes. We never cease to be amazed at how He connects us with contacts, donors, or ministry partners so the Good News can be spread throughout the world." ■

A Russian child, above, in the marketplace.

Opposite: Focus on the Family has worked with many translators and organizations to make resources available to help families throughout the world.

Below, just a few of the foreign translations of Dr. Dobson's book *When God Doesn't Make Sense*.

AFTERWORD

WHAT AN AMAZING TWENTY-FIVE YEARS IT HAS BEEN! It's one thing to believe that our God is faithful—as indeed He is—but it's quite another to experience His faithfulness, minute-by-minute and day-by-day. The pages of this book cannot begin to describe adequately just how steadfastly He has guided and protected us over the years. Looking back to where we've been, I'm optimistic about what lies ahead.

My prayer is that five, ten, and even another twenty-five years down the road, Focus on the Family's mission will be the same as it is today: to share the Good News of Jesus Christ with as many people as possible, and to accomplish that objective by preserving the institution of the family.

Indeed, nothing is more important than the message of the cross. Everything else pales in comparison. Each one of us has been born into sin, and in our unrighteous state we are unable to approach God or have a relationship with Him. That is why He sent His only Son, Jesus, to come to earth as a baby, to grow and live a sinless life, and to die on the cross on our behalf. Even though He was innocent, He allowed Himself to be humiliated, beaten, and crucified as a sacrifice for our sins.

But the story doesn't end with His death. On the third day, He rose from the grave, victorious over sin and death and Satan, in order that we might be reconciled to God. Through Jesus, our Heavenly Father has made it possible for us not only to have a relationship with Him, but also to enjoy the incredible benefits of eternal life. All we are required to do is confess our sins and acknowledge our need for Him, placing our trust in Jesus Christ and His finished work on the cross. What glorious news!

Even within this wonderful gospel message, God evokes the imagery of the family. Ephesians 1:5 tells us that "He destined us in love to be His sons through Jesus Christ (RSV)." And in numerous places throughout Scripture, God is described as our loving Heavenly Father. It isn't difficult to understand why the Lord holds the institution of the family in such high esteem. After all, He created it!

In the years ahead, as this ministry endeavors to strengthen and encourage families here on earth, may our ultimate goal continue to be ushering new members into the family of God. That is the only true achievement by which our success can be measured. Pray for us when our names come to mind. We are one in the bond of God's love.

James C. Dobson, Ph.D.
January 2002